D0268067

After the Fire

ALSO BY PAUL ZIMMER

The American Zimmer
The Ancient Wars
Big Blue Train
Crossing to Sunlight: Selected Poems
Earthbound Zimmer
Family Reunion: Selected and New Poems
The Great Bird of Love
Live with Animals
The Republic of Many Voices
The Ribs of Death
With Wanda: Town and Country Poems
The Zimmer Poems

After the Fire

A WRITER FINDS HIS PLACE

Paul Zimmer

University of Minnesota Press

Minneapolis / London

The University of Minnesota Press appreciates permission to reprint the following essays in this book. "Gardening" was originally published as "Sundays in the Garden" in *Crazy Horse* (June 2001). "The Blind World" (originally titled "The Blind World, Atomic Battlefields") and "The Condition of My Faith" were first published in *The Georgia Review.* "The Catcher," "Young Jazz," and "Strangers in Friendly Places" first appeared in *The Gettysburg Review* in 1999–2001, and are reprinted here with the acknowledgment of the editors. "Making Poetry" was originally published as "Demolition Diagrams" in *The Southern Review* 36, no. 2 (Spring 2000): 406–17. "Taking a Punch" was first published in *The Ohio Review* 61 (June 2000). "Dogs" was first published in *The Great River Review* 33 (Fall/Winter 2000–2001).

Excerpt from "Those Winter Sundays," by Robert Hayden, from *Angle of Ascent: New and Collected Poems,* by Robert Hayden. Copyright 1975, 1972, 1970, 1996 by Robert Hayden.

Published by the University of Minnesota Press
111 Third Avenue South, Suite 290
Minneapolis, MN 55401-2520
http://www.upress.umn.edu

Library of Congress Cataloging-in-Publication Data

Zimmer, Paul.
    After the fire : a writer finds his place / Paul Zimmer.
        p.   cm.
    ISBN 0-8166-4019-X
    1. Zimmer, Paul—Homes and haunts—Wisconsin.   2. Poets,
American—20th century—Biography.   3. Wisconsin—Social life and
customs.   4. Country life—Wisconsin.   I. Title.
PS3576.I47 Z463 2002
811'.54—dc21   2001006531

Printed in the United States of America on acid-free paper

The University of Minnesota is an equal-opportunity educator and employer.

12 11 10 09 08 07 06 05 04 03 02   10 9 8 7 6 5 4 3 2 1

To Suzanne, Justine, Erik, Margaret, Aaron, and Caroline

And, behold, the Lord passed by, and a great and strong wind
rent the mountains, and brake in pieces the rocks before the Lord,
but the Lord was not in the wind; and after the wind an earthquake,
but the Lord was not in the earthquake; and after the earthquake a fire,
but the Lord was not in the fire; and after the fire a still small voice.

I Kings 19:11–12

Contents

Acknowledgments

I AM GLAD to have this opportunity to express my gratitude to Hollins University, the University of Montana, and Wichita State University for salubrious appointments as visiting writer. These came at a very beneficial time for me, spiritually and financially, and were indispensable to me in completing this book.

Special thanks to great friends and readers, who helped me with my prose and details of this manuscript over the past several years, especially my sister, Beverly Hildebrand, Jim McKean, Gary Gildner, Brendan Galvin, Doug Armato, Bill Ford, Peter Stitt, Steve Corey, Ben Logan, Cliff Krainik, John McGowan, and to the cherished memory of Stanley Lindberg.

Prologue: Finding Home

After you have exhausted what there is in business, politics,
conviviality, love, and so on—have found that none of these
finally satisfy, or permanently wear—what remains? Nature
remains: to bring out from their torpid recesses the affinities of
a man or a woman with the open air—the sun by day and the
stars of heaven by night.

Walt Whitman

For some lost reason aeons ago, during the glacial period, the Patrician ice sheet split widely in its slow grind over the Midwest, separating at the top of an area in southwest Wisconsin. It passed down each side of the land to meet again at a base in northern Iowa, leaving a heart-shaped area of nearly fifteen thousand square miles open to the forces of weather.

In subsequent ages the wear of erosion on this place was gentler than the gigantic pressure and scraping of ice. Because this unglaciated area was formed by wind and rain, these "driftless" hills don't soar like mountains formed by upheavals of the earth's crust. They are uniform in height, no part looming much over another. The slopes are steep and abrupt in some places, especially at the end of ridges, but the countryside rolls high and handsome. In our valley the Kickapoo River glints and twists so crookedly through meadows and wooded areas that it takes many miles to progress a single mile.

This is where Suzanne and I bought our land a dozen years ago, in a region of hundred-year-old dairy farms and apple orchards. It was late summer the first time we drove the two-mile dirt road and saw the house on the end of the ridge with its view into the valley of farms sweeping below and rising again into distant green ridges.

Intending to buy only a cottage or small cabin and an acre or two of land, we assumed that only the house, outbuildings, and patch of land were included in the quoted sale price—which was twice what we had intended to pay. When the agent told us that over a hundred acres were also included in the package, we were awed and intimidated. But we immediately refused his offer to sell off the land for us.

I have been in love with Suzanne Koklauner for forty-four years. We have raised two children, lived together in four states, and resided briefly in half a dozen others. We met in college and, although our interests are widely divergent, we share, among other things, an abiding love of the countryside. Both of us grew up in Rust Belt mill towns. Our family houses had backyards the size of postage stamps. We had no conception of what an acre was—much less 117 acres. We could see that the land was beautiful, spacious, mysterious, and we wanted it. We didn't even bother to tour it before we hustled up our modest resources and wrote the check.

The house is one story with a deck overlooking the valley. It is plain, white, and efficient, with a separate two-car garage, which we have converted into our library. Just down the road is a steel Morton outbuilding where we keep tools, machines, and firewood. Eino Paasikivi, the original owner, cleared the area around the house so that the views into the valley are unobstructed. He had immigrated from Finland with his parents at an early age. He did all the work on the house himself, and his concept was very spare and functional. Most of his life he had worked as a mechanic and garage supervisor, and he was in his sixties when he was finally able to buy the land he wanted.

Paasikivi worked hard to create his own isolation. We bless him for his vision and energy. Eino wanted to be alone with his wife and his life. He told me that sometimes in the winter they would be snowed in for days before the plough made it through. He liked that, and so do we. Will Cobble, who lives down the hill from us on County Highway C, tells me that Paasikivi was friendly up to a point, but "really liked his privacy."

The Finn and his wife left us some furniture, an old Ford tractor, and assorted tools. We moved some of our own pieces up from Iowa City, along with a load of books and my typewriter. We bought a four-wheel-drive Toyota pickup truck and began a decade of weekend, vacation, and holiday commutes—three hours up and three hours back. The place grew to be the center of our lives, our home before it was our home. The beauty and isolation became more idealized in our thoughts as the years went on, and this made commuting more difficult. Three years ago I retired and we moved in full time, no longer having to endure the pain of departure.

The very first, magical day on our ridge a dozen years ago, we were treated to a classic driftless hills morning. It began with low fog shimmering, filling the valley, and the quarter day moon in the pristine sky above. Then the fog lifted, burning away to reveal fields, woods, and the Kickapoo River looping through the valley. Later in the day we were regaled by the sky. There was a brief shower in the afternoon, and when it cleared we walked down the road. We stopped to look back down the ridge and, God is my witness, a rainbow arched over the house—an invocation, a complete, full-colored bow spread vividly over the roof. We accepted it as a sign.

I first read Henry David Thoreau's *Walden* in 1955; I was twenty-one years old and highly impressionable. He begins famously, "When I wrote the following pages, or rather the bulk of them, I lived alone, in the woods, a mile from any neighbor, in a house which I had built myself, on the shore of Walden Pond, in Concord, Massachusetts, and earned my living by the labor of my hands only." Thoreau was a young man when he wrote *Walden*. Early in the book he says, "Old deeds for old people, and new deeds for new . . . I have lived some thirty years on this planet, and I have yet to hear the first syllable of valuable or even earnest advice from my seniors. They have told me nothing, and probably cannot tell me anything to the purpose. Here is life, an experiment to a great extent untried by me; but it does not avail me that they have tried it. If I have any experience which I think valuable, I am sure to reflect that this my Mentors said nothing about."

As I read this in 1955 I almost rose to my feet and cheered, but as I copy it down now, I am in my midsixties and remain in my chair. Like the mass of men, I have not infrequently led what Thoreau called "a life of quiet desperation." But I cannot imagine less desperation had I dropped out and chosen what seemed an easier path. It has been forty-six years since I read *Walden* the first time. Perhaps I have given too much away and waited too long to retreat to this isolation, but I embrace it now and will not be ashamed or denied my brief, happy time with it. My great regret is that I could not come to it sooner.

I do not exaggerate when I say that Suzanne and I go for weeks without speaking to anyone but each other and our dog. We wave to Richie Halverson or Jake Yant, our neighbors, as they work in a distant field, or we nod to the grocer as we shop occasionally in town. We speak regularly on the telephone to our children and grandchildren, and to distant friends. We have visitors from time to time. I write and receive many letters. But we are blessedly alone on our ridge.

Sometimes I stop in my tracks and look, empty-headed, as I gaze at the meadows and woods. Grand thoughts are not necessary. The stillness is sublime. Thoreau wrote of the hours of silence around Walden Pond, "I grew in those seasons like corn in the night, and they were far better than work of the hand would have been. They were not subtracted from my life, but so much over and above my usual allowance." Even after some years of being here in the silence, it still amazes me. I am constantly surprised by the hush. Perhaps these years won't be subtracted from my life—or at least my aging will be moderated. In any event, I have the rest of my life now to cherish silence. I have no inclination anymore to tell young people things they don't want to hear. Old deeds for old people.

After the Fire

Strangers in Friendly Places

I HAD JUST TURNED into a scrawny, ardent seven-year-old in 1941 when the United States entered the Second World War. Everyone was very worried about the conflict. My mother's parents were French and Belgian immigrants, and my father of German ancestry, but they did not clash over the war. We were apprehensive that it might come to America, to our town of many factories. My father was on our neighborhood Civil Defense team and patrolled with a red-filtered flashlight during the practice blackouts while we sat in our darkened basement and my mother taught us French songs like "Frère Jacques" and "Alouette."

Each summer during the 1940s, we made trips from Canton, Ohio, to Linton, Indiana, to visit my mother's parents. It seemed like a journey to France. The trip was long, eight hours, about as long as it takes to fly to Paris from Chicago today. Some of the roads were still dirt and gravel. We got up before dawn, and often it was foggy. By the time we drove into Linton in the late afternoon, I was ready to jump out of my skin.

We all crowded happily into my grandparents' little house. The old chairs, couch, and tables in the living room were deco-rated with lace doilies and hand-knit afghans. On top of the upright piano was a bowl of anise candy, peppermints, nougats, and a stereoscope viewer with a box of double-image cards of Notre Dame, Lourdes, a castle on a hilltop rising above French fields, and other scenes of France. On the flowery papered walls were reproductions of *The Angelus,* a Rousseau land-scape, and a little girl gazing up at a bluebird in a tree. There was a windup phonograph and a stack of Maurice Chevalier records. Everything seemed quaint and "French."

I was allowed into my grandparents' bedroom only once, when I was helping my *grand-père* look for something. I remember old photographs of French and Belgian relatives on the tops of heavy dressers, a mirror that had started to peel around its edges, and a bed covered with a chenille spread on which rested a French doll with auburn hair and taffeta dress. My *grand-père* took down a box from his closet and gave me a chocolate-covered cherry. It was a privilege, a secret, and I did not brag to my sister.

A Monarch cooking stove sat in the corner of the kitchen along with a bucket of coal and a small kerosene stove used in very hot weather. Nearby was a white enameled table where foods were prepared and dished up. Cooking was a hot job in the summer. My *grand-mère* always had a pot simmering on a back burner and kept a towel by the stove to dry her face. Only cold water flowed from the faucets, and she heated kettles for washing and baths. She worked constantly—cooking, sweep-ing, washing dishes, putting things away—when we visited, assisted by my mother, sister, and aunts. At the end of the day, she sat in exhausted silence on the porch as the others talked. At the side of the house she kept a flower garden planted with daisies, carnations, moss roses.

She indulged me. As I was the youngest and last grand-child, I was allowed to fire my cap pistol outside the house and clutter the front yard with orange crates I had torn apart to build wagons and hideaways. Once she helped me make a bow and arrow out of branches. My mother was amazed at her tolerance.

We all used the two-hole outhouse at the back of the garden. I did not like it, and there were always bees threatening me as I sat. Once a week the iceman came in his horse-drawn wagon, lugged in, with tongs, a big, dripping block, and dropped it with a thud into a tray beside the icebox. *Chink-chuck,* he halved it expertly with his pick, heaving the pieces up into the insulated cabinet. I followed him back out to his wagon and he handed me a chip of ice, gritty with splinters from the old floorboards. I wiped it carefully before putting it in my mouth.

Chickens and a few rabbits were kept out back in small pens near a large storage shed. My *grand-père* was proud of his vegetable garden. It took up the whole fenced backyard—leeks, shallots, tomatoes, potatoes, carrots, herbs, green beans, peas, parsnips, onions, lettuce, radishes, usually a patch of sweet corn. A grape arbor was decorated with my *grand-père*'s whittlings—profiles of family members back in France. He used a tobacco spray to control pests, and my sister and I helped him pick off tomato and potato worms. I sat by him on a stool in the back entry porch as he trimmed vegetables and rinsed them in a bucket of water. He gripped his worn pocket-knife in the palm of his knobby, freckled hand and talked as he worked. He spoke my name differently—not *Pall* but *Powell,* sounding the vowels higher and rolling the *l* a little.

Sometimes on summer nights, he would take me out to his garden and hold my hand as we looked up at the sky together. Having toiled all his adult life in the coal mines of France and America, he liked to stand out under the stars. He told me the names of the planets and explained their places—Pluton, Saturne, Mercure, Mars—how Earth is a planet, too, and we all circle the sun. I fancy my small hand in his made him remember his boyhood before he ran away from the conscription in

France. He hated the war and worried about his people. His hometown, Mericourt, was destroyed by the Germans in the First World War because of its coal mines. Sometimes he told me a little of his sadness. When I fetched small, pale blue letters from the mailbox for him, he read them eagerly. Even as a child I could sense his yearning. He had left his home forever. I could not imagine such a thing. It made me afraid to think about it—the brave decision he and his family made, knowing that they would probably never see each other again. The most difficult good-bye. He did not find the rich life of opportunity he had imagined in America, but he also did not become a bloody corpse on a remote European battlefield.

My *grand-mère* came from southern, French-speaking Belgium, and she and my *grand-père* met in America. She never saw her family again either. They raised seven children and lost two in infancy to what they sadly referred to as "summer complaint." My mother told me a story of how my *grand-père* once said good-bye to them and rode the rods from Utah to Indiana pursuing a mining job. When I seemed surprised— my dignified French *grand-père* riding under a boxcar like a hobo—she looked at me and said, "You weren't exactly born with a silver spoon in your mouth."

In the little Indiana frame house, six of us sat at table. If aunts and uncles came, there were two sittings, and the men ate first. There was always soup before dinner and a little paté. The main course was meat—beef brisket, fried and stewed chicken or rabbit, or ham in green beans—then creamed new potatoes, onions or leeks, and vegetables. There were big sweating pitchers of iced tea. The adults had a glass of wine. Cheese and bread were served at the end. Occasionally my *grand-mère* made chocolate pie for my sister and me, but usually I was allowed to turn the crank of the ice-cream freezer while the adults had coffee.

After dinner we sat on the front porch with fans and fly-swatters. Uncle Joe made a clapper for me out of two boards and a piece of leather, so I could make noise and keep the blackbirds out of the elms in the front yard. I was enthusiastic in my work, and soon everyone regretted that he had given me this assignment.

Some evenings, especially when there were visiting relatives, we went inside and gathered around the piano to sing while my mother played. My favorites were "Over There," "When Yankee Doodle Learned to Parlez-Vous Français," "Joan of Arc," and "Nola."

We went to bed when things cooled down a bit, slept on cots or mattresses placed on the floor, with electric fans whirring and clanking. One night I was on a feather bed in a corner of the living room, hot and uncomfortable, listening to the rumbling sleep of the adults. At one point I got up, crept across the room, and struck a resounding key on the piano. The snoring stopped momentarily, and my sister sat up in her cot. I dropped down to the floor and squirmed back to my feather bed. "Paul!" my sister whispered admonishingly. Shortly the thrum and glottal buzz resumed over the whir of the fans.

Our departures were always emotional. My grandparents did not like to say *au revoir,* so we moved quickly, having packed the car the night before. We waved and waved good-bye as we drove away down the street. On one of our return journeys we were sideswiped by another car in the early morning mist, and our luggage was smashed on the running board, clothes and gift vegetables strewn down the road. My sister and I wept and held each other as we watched our parents gather up our belongings.

Many things drop away, but memories of those summer visits to Indiana abide with me. There was a French accent on everything. My mother taught me to be proud of this. She had never been to France, but her enthusiasm was infectious; she sang "The Marseillaise" at the drop of a hat. She teased my father about being a "kraut," but they did not argue as the war raged. We all rejoiced with her when France was liberated in 1945. When she was angry with one of us, she said, "You're getting my French up!" She used French words and phrases in her conversation.

The regret any halfway-civilized American feels over not having learned French is a condition of advanced adulthood. When Suzanne and I go to France, although my pleasure is intense, I feel deficient. What I remember most of my grand-parents' house are the tones of that sonorous language, so pleasing to my ear: my mother talking to my grandparents in French and them speaking to us in English with heavy accents, the vowels sliding into each other and the consonants round-ing. These were the sounds of comfort and family, the home I have tried to keep all my life.

Puivert is a tiny French village of four hundred people in southern Languedoc. Suzanne and I have the good fortune to have a modest house to visit there. The upland countryside echoes the fields and sky of southwest Wisconsin, where we live most of the year, near Soldiers Grove, a small town approx-imately the same size as Puivert. Both of these landscapes are rolling, but the slopes that rise from the valley in France are the soaring foothills of the Pyrenees. The soil in the French fields is tawny rather than dark brown; the houses and out-buildings in the distant hamlets and farms are built on ancient medieval sites and made of the buff-colored stones of the area, in contrast to the wooden frame white houses and red barns of new world Wisconsin. In both places we are surrounded by wooded hills and valley meadows.

Our good fortune amazes us—to be finishing our lives in these two verdant places, to have a home in Wisconsin and a place to visit in France, five thousand miles apart. These are the kind of scenes we dreamt about during all our working years in cities and towns. Our luck was not calculated. The opportunities to have these places came by chance, and we thank the gods that we turned the corner, saw them, and were able to act when they presented themselves.

In Puivert we share our small eighteenth-century stone house with the writers Susan Ludvigson and Scott Ely, who pioneered the property years ago. It was Susan who purchased the shambles originally and, working slowly with local artisans, made it pleasantly livable—then had the grace and generosity to allow us to become co-owners. It is a row house in a narrow lane, the site at least two hundred years old, in a *hameau* called Campsadourny just a short stroll from Puivert. On each side of our house are shells of abandoned structures, now occupied by birds and mice. If you turn left leaving our door, you are headed toward the village and a view of the castle on the hill above the valley. If you turn right you walk into the fields and farmland surrounded by the beginnings of the mountain range.

We own no land, only the house, but behind it is a vegetable garden maintained by three elderly French people who live down the way. They waddle and bend arthritically to tend the tidy rows each day, chattering to each other. Gazing down from our beveled second-story window, I recall my *grand-père*'s garden—so sumptuous, orderly, and necessary, like the lines of a good poem. When we lean out and express admiration to the elders for their *jardin,* small gifts begin to appear on our doorstep—bags of onions and potatoes, bundles of lettuce, heads of cabbage, bouquets of broccoli and cauliflower.

In Puivert there is a small grocery store, a *boulangerie,* a café, two good restaurants, an antique bridge over a small stream with a *pissoir* in the middle through which you can pee directly into the current, a *musée* of the territory, and a troubadour castle high on a hill above the town. Like our Wisconsin farm, it is a quiet place, but in Soldiers Grove there is no museum, French bakery, or castle on the hill, and the restaurants serve hamburgers, pizza, fried fish, and broasted chicken.

One year we arrive in southern France in early October to stroll in still-green forests and fields, leaving behind a harvested Wisconsin landscape already russet and yellow with a distinct autumnal snap in the air. In France it is warm. The birds have only begun to flock, and crops are still standing in the fields. Our rough stone three-story house sits in a narrow lane of seven occupied and two derelict houses. It is perhaps a good deal older than we think. When it was being restored, a large, heart-shaped ancient stone, big as a semi wheel, was discovered buried in the foundation (what Scott Ely refers to as the world's heaviest valentine) with a kind of fleur-de-lis (which might be a Basque symbol) and a pansylike four-leaf flower expertly carved into circles in the gray stone—curious signs giving some indication that there could have been a dwelling on the site much earlier. Perhaps it marked the grave of two old lovers or celebrated a marriage. Whatever its purpose, the stone was meant to endure. It is now propped against the second-floor wall across from the bed, a symbol for us of love immemorial.

As in our Wisconsin home, the farms in the valley are dairy and cattle farms, and the fields are planted with grasses, grains, and corn, or used for pasture. We note differences between French and Wisconsin farmers. French farmers favor enclosed trucks instead of the open American pickup. Wisconsin farmers bale their hay and are very careful to make certain that corncobs and oats are completely dried out before harvesting. The French farmers in our valley grind everything—corn, cobs, stocks, and whole grasses—into small, damp shreds, which are pressed and stored under tarpaulins weighed down with discarded tires. They harvest the large fields as though conducting tank warfare. They use John Deere tractors with formidable shooting grinders and big hauling trucks running alongside to catch the ground-up crops. The noise is immense as the vehicles move back and forth, and in the distance, as always for eight centuries, the castle on the distant hillside overlooks the harvesting.

Built early in the twelfth century as a Cathar stronghold, the castle was burned and looted in 1210 by the righteous Christian knights sent by Pope Innocent III to exterminate the heretics. In the thirteenth century the troubadours built, contiguous to the ruins, a new structure devoted to the bardic life. The English version of the castle brochure says, "Poet gatherings were frequent in Puivert." Evidently this was true even when the Cathars occupied the castle. There exists a fragment of a satirical poem, dating from 1170, written in the langue d'oc, which translates: "This verse was composed to the sound of bagpipes / At Puivert among songs and laughter."

The landscape in Languedoc is romantic and "poetic." It amazes us always to be driving in the countryside and suddenly come around a turn to see another world, a magnificent chateau, a fortified tower, or a splendid ancient church in a town of ancient houses. A town like Mirepoix at first seems dreary, lined with mud-colored stone row houses and stucco facades, then we turn a corner and come into a delightful medieval square, shops fronted in centuries-old buildings. On the narrow side streets there are entryways and antique doors leading to the chambers and apartments of the residents. In warm weather the doors and ground-level windows are left open. The apartments behind these antique facades are lovely, elegant—and very French.

Years ago I was paging through a book of photogravures of old Paris and doing some French dreaming. The antiquity and depth in an image of a passageway leading to Balzac's house drew me in. So much energy and history had passed along these worn stones. I wanted very much to be in such a place. Now we come across such venerable nooks regularly in our rambles.

The first time we traveled to France, almost thirty years ago, we drove out of Paris through old neighborhoods into the countryside. It seemed to me that the country was impoverished. The dingy, ancient row houses would have been slum neighborhoods in Pittsburgh, where we lived at the time. It was puzzling: the people seemed prosperous and chic as they walked their tatty streets. I had no sense of what *old* meant. In America we do not treasure old things. We obliterate them. But when I had glimpses into the French houses, I realized how rich and rare the interiors were, how sophisticated and meaningful, so much tradition and elegance behind the old and seemingly crumbled facades. France is not a condemnable slum. It is antiquity. People live in the cities with true grace among the artifacts of the past, within their own history, cherishing their traditions.

Strong measures and regulations are used to preserve the venerable French countryside. So far there are no double-wide trailers or prefabricated houses, as there are in Wisconsin, scourging the landscape. But blinking communications towers spring up among the trees on wooded hillsides and mountains; television dishes mushroom everywhere; garish signage is increasing. France is alluring, and regular visitors like us become proprietary, but what right do *we* have to be worried and offended by encroachment—we who are strangers in this country, visitors with only distant, faded familial ties? I have observed with frustration and sadness some of the irretrievable, heedless cultural losses in our own country over the past six decades. Only a few things are left of the simple artifacts that were in my grandparents' house in Indiana. Apparently everything was sold or thrown away. I wish I had the stereoscope, the candy dish, or my *grand-père*'s worn French pocket-knife. Somehow I did end up with his gold watch and its handsome inscription:

Presented
To
J.J. Surmont
By
Local 2134
U.M.W. of A.

I also have my mother's pride and a small stake in France.

At the local Musée du Quercorb in Puivert they show a video clip filmed in the castle, depicting a thirteenth century troubadour entertainment. People dance, joining hands and skipping; there is a great deal of shouting and singing, plucking at lutes, pounding of tambours; a highly animated juggler tosses fire batons. All the while, dour-looking, aristocratic Catholic administrators oversee tables laden with food and great jars of wine. It makes me wonder what else these people did with themselves. Troubadours are always depicted in a festive mode. Did they just sing songs and prance all the time? They were aristocrats, landowners, upper crust, I surmise. The real people, the rustics and workers, lived below the walls, around the lake and in the wooded valley. These were the artisans and laborers who built the castle: they raised food—grains, sheep, goats— and they fished the lake, supplying food to the nobles. Hunting was reserved for the aristocracy. If the area was under assault, the serfs had the right to hustle up the hill to the castle and were let in through a small door in the wall.

The castle is imposing on the hill, a cluster of square towers and stone walls visible from every angle in the valley. We never tire of looking at it, in sun or moonlight. We try to imagine what the area looked like in medieval times. The lake just outside of Puivert was larger and covered much of the valley. The fields were forests. The foothills probably looked much as they do now, except perhaps where pastures run partway up into the rises. The silence must have been omnipresent, except for the occasional barking of dogs, the bleating of sheep, rooster cries, and the fussing of blackbirds—the sounds we hear today, along with the bread truck honking in the lane or the passage of an occasional vehicle. At night probably only scattered fires were visible, and perhaps some revelry from the castle or the distant howling of wolves could be heard.

The French still don't like to light up the darkness in their countryside. Windows are shuttered at night, and each hamlet and farm in our valley has but one street lamp, as if it were the signal fire. Occasionally car or truck lights move down one of the back roads, but the rural French, at least in Languedoc, still move outdoors at night by the light of the moon.

Puivert itself is sparsely lighted by just a few street lamps, unlike small towns in the United States. From our hilltop in Wisconsin, we can see the outskirts of Soldiers Grove in the distance, lit up with lines of yellow streetlights, which glow over the area like candles on a birthday cake. In the distance the horizon glows over Readstown, Viroqua, Seneca, and Gays Mills.

The history and prehistory of Soldiers Grove and the unglaciated hills of southwestern Wisconsin are not as extended and involved as that of Puivert and Languedoc, and the record of events is much skimpier. From the sixteenth through the eighteenth centuries this country was part of "Nouvelle France," and there are traces of this heritage in the names of many of the towns: Prairie du Chien, La Crosse, Eau Claire, Fond du

Lac. Before then, tribes of Sauk, Fox, Sioux, Potawatomi, Chippewa, Kickapoo, and other native Americans roamed the area, hunting and fighting skirmishes with each other among the rises and valleys, but their triumphs and failures are unrecorded.

The little town of Soldiers Grove, about four miles from our farm, is situated in a hollow beside the Kickapoo River, which has a long history of ruinous flooding. In 1978, after a major flood destroyed much of the town, the business district was moved to higher ground east of the river. An embankment was created and the old decimated business section made into a park. Because its buildings were designed to use solar energy, the new business area—a grocery, motel and restaurant, bar, filling station, hardware store, drugstore, and other assorted shops and services—was dubbed Solar Town, U.S.A. Grown a little shabby after more than twenty years of hard weather, it was the first such area in the country to utilize the energy of the sun.

The citizens remain perky and devoted, although the living is not always easy. Small dairy farming is not a growth business these days, and the per capita income of Crawford County is one of the lowest in the state. Many of the remaining fine old houses in town have grown shabby, and there are sections of trailer houses, installed probably before zoning could be reestablished after the flood.

The farms in the Kickapoo area are mostly well kept, but with the decline of the small dairy business, the scenic coun-tryside is beginning to be developed by realtors for recreation. Summerhouses and cabins are being built along the river and on some of the ridges. Eino Passikivi built our tidy, two-bed-room house thirty years ago, purchasing parts of several seasoned farms to create an L-shaped property over the ridge and down the wooded hillsides. We have discovered that he leveled, burned, and bulldozed an old farmhouse and outbuildings, leaving only square, sunken traces. We don't know why he did this; perhaps he wanted to obliterate antiquity, wanted clean Finnish isolation, and had no feeling for the old life that was lived here. We cherish his scheme for being alone but wish he had left more of the past for us to regard.

People from this area sometimes refer to themselves as living in the trees. It is a lilting countryside, wooded ridges rising uniformly out of the cultivated valleys. From the ridge tops the vistas are long. From ours we see down through woods to the Kickapoo River, famous for its crookedness, twisting through the meadows, to distant hills and farm silhouettes.

The Kickapoo tribe was the early dominant tenant of the area and the word *Kickapoo* in the Algonquin language means something like "he goes here, then goes there." The Kickapoo were a bellicose bunch, raiders of lands far from their villages; they would hire themselves out for dirty work to the French, British, and Spanish. They were also hunters and capable farmers, raising corn, beans, and squash. They did not take well to European influences and kept their own customs. For some reason they pulled out of this area just before our Revolutionary War and headed south, leaving the land open for the hunting forays and skirmishes of other tribes.

There are large, ancient mounds in the area, built by native Americans, formed in the shape of animals. In Crawford County are the Kickapoo Indian Caverns, and there are other caves throughout southwestern Wisconsin, including some recently discovered in the Kickapoo valley and along the banks of the Mississippi. The caves, marked with drawings of hunters and animals dating back a thousand years, were evidently important places of refuge for prehistoric Indians and animals.

In south central France are many caves full of magnificent paintings and markings made by Paleolithic artists, giving more graphic hints of the prehistory of the area. Lascaux, discovered in 1940, is most famous, but other gallery caves have been located, including the masterful renderings of lions, bison, and bears in the Grotte de Chauvet, first explored in 1994 and only recently being documented.

Near Puivert is the Grotte de Niaux, one of the few caves open to the public. It is a chill spring day when we nervously enter, mincing our way on the damp, slippery floor as our lamp beams sway. The cave has been explored by spelunkers for centuries. The spectacular stalactites and stalagmites in the entry chambers have mostly been broken off as souvenirs, and we see only their stumps. But the first large chamber is immense and less violated, the ceiling so high the beams of our lanterns cannot reach it. Our silence is reverential.

Farther in we begin to see graffiti, some in fancy French script dating back to the mid-seventeenth century. We duck through several small passageways and begin a descent through a long open area into the *salon noir.* Here the guide stops and asks us to switch off our lanterns and gather where she stands with her light. We bump into each other and chuckle as we grope toward her. She is speaking in French as she turns the spot of her light on a painting of a bison. There are sighs and soft exclamations, then profound silence as she plays her light over the painting and others surrounding it.

The skill of the drawings, made eleven thousand years ago, is immediately evident. The artists worked with unfaltering confidence. Like all great art it suggests as much as it shows. There are no pictures of human figures in any of the caves, only astonishingly skillful images of animals. The guide shows us horses, stags, ibises, and more bison, some overlapping, some with arrows or barbs in their sides. I am struck by the vitality of the drawing and by the use of perspective and shading techniques thought to have been developed only in the last few centuries.

These are not decorative sketches. The art is life. The eyes of the animals seem to see. There are no bad or indifferent drawings. All of them are accomplished and necessary. My own artistic abilities are primitive at best; I could not think of making sketches as meaningful and good. The animals bound and turn, one crossing another with marvelous energy. The paintings are a tribute to the animals—the fear of them and need for them. The artists were brave, practiced creators, feeling compelled to enter deep into the disquieting darkness of the earth and crawl into uncomfortable corners in order to record respect and reverence for the lives and deaths of these creatures that were so necessary to their existence.

Possibly the artists realized that in these drawings, as in the carving of the stone in our house in Puivert, they were leaving something that would endure beyond their lives. Dream animals in a dark place. They must have observed the bodies of humans and animals deteriorating to nothing after death—would the pictures make the spirits of animals abide so that they would continue to feed their people? The guide shows us that they even did preliminary drafting before making their compelling final versions. Eleven millennia ago! The artistry and care are staggering.

There are marks in other sections of the cave—dots, notches, lines in red and black, all precisely drawn. No one knows their meaning. Are they directions, accounts, numberings, timekeeping, records of reoccurrence, astronomical notes? Obviously they bear great significance, perhaps to things outside the cave: stars, seasons, animal kills, lives lost, life cycles, or events beyond our comprehension.

Entering the cave I felt claustrophobic, yet in the very large chambers there is an assuasive sense of openness, as if one is under a shrouded night sky. What must it have been like when the stalagmites were still intact, the first explorers picking their way through them into the abyss with a palm torch? Courage and determination were characteristics embodied by these people. They had no words for these qualities, but in our distant admiration and wonder, we can name them.

We see only a small portion of the art at Niaux. We are told there is much more in deeper chambers, some of it in almost inaccessible places. The drawings we see on the moist, peach-colored cave walls seem rendered on living skin, the uterus of the earth, the womb from which all things are born.

Languedoc has always been a remote, maverick part of France, especially this deep southern part. Far away from courts and kings, it is rarely mentioned in history books. Yet from what we can determine in our faltering translations and reading of meager texts in English, beyond the agricultural and market life its simple human history seems sad and deeply involved to us.

Ruins of Cathar castles on the remotest, most inaccessible crags and peaks in the area are astonishing to behold. These strange, ascetic people must have been part mountain goat. Obviously they had a great deal to fear, building in such precarious places. Marauding crusaders, who were promised indulgences and booty by the pope, swept down from Lyon and relentlessly assaulted their high strongholds. In true Languedocien dissident tradition, the Cathars were frequently supported by local Catholics, and the conflict often came down to southern resistance to northern influence. But the crusaders pressed on. These pious thugs were complete in their slaughter and destruction. They mutilated and burned the Cathar priests, called *Perfects,* and butchered any lay believers who refused to renounce the faith. When the dirty work was completed, an inquisition was formed by the Catholic church to investigate and persecute the survivors. Almost nothing remains of the beliefs and customs of the Cathars, at one time a thriving, preeminent group in Languedoc.

The early residents of Crawford County, Wisconsin, do not have such a dramatic legacy of zealous hatred, suspicion, and persecution—unless you figure they drove the Indian tribes out of the area to make it safe for Christianity. I am not aware of a synagogue or a mosque anywhere in the area. The pretty church steeples scattered through the countryside mark various and dwindling congregations: Methodist, Presbyterian, Catholic, Baptist, and Lutheran. The local newspapers are full of news about church suppers and festivities. The activities seem benign and apathetic.

As in southern Languedoc, the ethnic blend in our Wisconsin area is bland. I have seen one black man living in each area. They are both—the American and the Frenchman—lonely joggers. When I pass them on the road, they never look up. There are a few Asians maintaining restaurants, a small group of Hispanic farm workers, and we note some Vietnamese refugees in both places.

Crawford County is beautiful. Created in 1818, it stretches north and east over five hundred square miles from the county seat at Prairie du Chien, on the Mississippi. Soldiers Grove was settled in the 1850s after the "war in the forest" cooled down and the Indians had been harassed to lands beyond the Mississippi. The town initially was called Pine Grove for the white pines prevalent in those days; the name was changed to Soldiers Grove in 1867 to honor some soldiers who camped in the area during the Black Hawk War—one of our nation's most shameful episodes of genocide—which swept through the area in 1832. Black Hawk, the great, eloquent Sauk leader, his tribe decimated by wars with the Sioux and difficulties with aggressive white settlers, brought his tribe from Iowa into Illinois, where he hoped to receive support from other tribes in a resettlement of the area. He did not receive this backup and found himself stranded with his people, strangers in an unfriendly place. Black Hawk sent emissaries to the whites to parley his situation, but the soldiers attacked his envoys, killing and scalping one of them.

Appalled by this outrage, Black Hawk had little choice. He attacked a superior white force, causing serious casualties, then began a hasty retreat toward Minnesota through southwestern Wisconsin. His band was pursued by a large force of volunteers and regulars, led by General Henry Atkinson. During the retreat the Indians came across the land where our farm is situated four miles outside of Soldiers Grove. It must have been a hard, terrified scramble for the little band—reduced now mostly to a handful of braves, women, and children—over these wooded ridges as they pressed on toward the Mississippi. Finally they were trapped at the confluence of the Bad Axe and Mississippi Rivers, where they attempted unsuccessfully to parley again. A gunboat came upriver from Prairie du Chien and Black Hawk's people were driven into the water, where sharpshooters picked them off as if they were a flock of ducks. The butchery went on for hours.

Clearly General Atkinson was not entirely in control of the situation in that bloodletting, and things got away from him. Yet I doubt that he felt any more shame or compassion than did the young troopers who were plugging away at the Sauks struggling in the currents. Racial hatred had boiled over, pity was absent, and the slaughter became blood lust. The Sauks who made it across the water were killed by their adversaries the Sioux, who had been alerted by the whites. Of the 1,200 Sauks who began the retreat, only 150 survived. The rabble troops were as complete in their genocide of the Sauks as the crusaders in southern France were in decimating the Cathars. In both of our peaceful, beguiling landscapes are historic sites of murderous immolation—what we refer to these days as ethnic cleansing.

We note on marble monuments in the squares of Languedocien villages that our area in France contributed many young lives to the carnage of the First World War. I imagine the same was true of all the other wars fought by France since the heretical Cathars were neutralized by righteous crusaders eight centuries ago. Remote agricultural areas have always been a source of bodies in times of war.

The Hundred Years' War, the brutal Thirty Years' War, the War of the Austrian Succession, Frederick the Great's Seven Years' War, the bloody Revolution, then Napoleon campaigning ruthlessly into the nineteenth century. He lost 50,000 men on one day in October 1813, fighting at Leipzig, and abandoned 200,000 to their fates. A month later he asked for the conscription of 300,000 more men, then lost 60,000 of them at Waterloo. Even after Bonaparte it went on and on. My *grand-père* was running away from being conscripted into the Franco-Prussian War when he escaped to America in 1870 and ended up in Indiana.

The history of the area around Puivert during the Second World War is murky. There are scattered tales of the heroic resistance of the Maquis of Picaussel, French guerilla resistance fighters who fought from hiding places in the high forests of the Plateau du Sault just south of Puivert. Supplied by Allied airdrops, they gave the Nazis fits, holding up convoys and detaining large troop movements as the time for the invasion approached. When members of the Maquis were captured, they paid mortally and publicly. The Germans burned one nearby village to the ground, gunning down citizens in retribution for the activity of the resisters.

Strolling near Puivert one Sunday morning, we heard voices from a loudspeaker in the square. As we approached, an old man was playing a wobbly military tattoo on an ancient heralding instrument. A small, somber group of citizens in their midseventies and older had gathered, and several men took turns hobbling to the microphone to testify. Two bent, hoary men stood proudly holding tricolor flags propped from their belts. We understood little, but could make out words like *maquis, courageux, assaut, dangereux, mort.* It was a dignified, resolute gathering of elderly men and women with just a scattering of younger people, obviously children and grandchildren of the freedom fighters. It was a fair, late Sunday morning, but shutters were still pulled on the houses that stood facing the square.

They noticed us as we stood off from their group. When they concluded their ceremony, they put on a scratchy record-ing of an old band pumping out "The Marseillaise" and sang vigorously. We mouthed the words with them. Then they bowed their heads for a moment of silence. Suzanne wept, and I struggled to maintain my composure. When it was over some men put the loudspeaker into a truck, and all of them shuffled into the *mairie*—the town hall—where champagne was being poured. They brought their glasses out into the sunlight, made toasts, and talked quietly. Several of them, people we had met in the village, beckoned to us to join them, but we shyly declined.

In Soldiers Grove some of the citizens still promote a military ambience. It is not forgotten that much of the land was origi-nally owned by veterans of the War of 1812, who were given property instead of money for their service. Like the agricul-tural areas of France, this rural area has always been a fruitful source of recruits in wartime. Farm boys are credulous and serviceable. There is evidence of this in the two war memorials in the city park, and in the tank parked in the yard of the American Legion building across the road from Solar Town, its cannon pointing at the local motel.

Several years ago members of the Legion promoted a cele-bration called Medal of Honor Day. Beauford T. Anderson, a Second World War Medal honoree, hails from Soldiers Grove, and there is a Medal of Honor Memorial Wall in the park. A committee was formed, and all living Medal of Honor winners were invited to a celebration. Every convertible in the area was commandeered for the parade, and each recipient had a chariot to ride in. The high school bands paraded, honking and squeaking patriotic marches, followed by some Second World War GIs in one rank, bearing a flag and grinding along arthritically like the First World War vets in Memorial Day parades when I was a kid. Korean War vets were next, and in only slightly better trim. The group of Gulf War participants marched perfectly in step, wearing snappy boots with yellow laces. At the end—at a distance from the others—strolling together casually in T-shirts and jeans, came the Vietnam vets. The black man we see jogging on the roads was among them, bearing an American flag. They were smiling and waving to people, fully aware of the symbol they were presenting. The crowd grew silent as they passed, not quite knowing how to react after the passage of so much honor and glory. Suzanne was weeping again, and I was swallowing hard.

A young American woman and her French husband have moved into a little house in Campsaure, the *hameau* just down the road from Puivert. Recently married, in their twenties, she is a talented painter and he builds fine chairs, couches, and ottomans. We sometimes see them on our walks and have exchanged visits with them. I admire and envy their youth and intensity, the dewiness of their vision, the verve with which they regard things.

The first time we visited France, I was in my late thirties and had more snap in my step than I have now. We came over to Paris for a week after a business trip to London, bringing the kids with us, driving into the countryside to visit Chartres. I was enchanted, recalling my heritage. I had done a lot of French dreaming, reading Balzac, Zola, Flaubert, Gide, Baudelaire, Rimbaud, Camus, gazing at books of photographs and volumes of impressionist paintings. I kept seeing people on the streets who looked like my grandparents, my aunts and uncles, and my mother. After the long, exhausting days of

touring, when we finally had the kids in bed, I wrote in a journal by lamplight in our hotel room.

I found that old journal and read it the other day. It is full
of the sights, tastes, sounds, smells, and textures of the places
we visited. There are verve and dewiness in the vision. I don't
know who that writer was. All the cells in my body have changed
a number of times since then. These words may not embody
that kind of freshness and excitement—at my age I am more
restrained, but I am well practiced and organized. I miss the
old fervor, but I am fortunate now to have more time to relish
and reflect on experiences and preserve some of the past. I
have learned to be selective. At times I wish I were thirty years
younger, so I could put it all down with that old sense of wonder. But I am here now with still enough energy, joy, and the
modest means to go on experiencing these landscapes and
savoring the memories. After forty years of working in offices,
it is a luxury. It is mostly an American dream, but it is a French
dream, too.

Who are we when we are in France? Property owners,
American barbarians, happy observers from Wisconsin. I am
a grandson of France, a lost Frenchman twice removed. If my
grandfather had stayed in France and survived conscription,
I would not have existed. Except—what if he had met my
grandmother waiting on tables in Lille instead of Sunnyside,
Utah? Supposing their seven children had been born in France?
But then my mother would not have met my father, so I still
would not have been me, but half of me, perhaps a product of
a different union. I would be a Frenchman, retired now, playing *boules* in the park and sitting on a bench under the
sycamores chatting with other old men. What would I have
been? A schoolteacher? Merchant? Priest? A miner like my
grandfather and uncles? Would I have been a poet? Would I
have beautiful children like Erik and Justine, a spouse as dear
as Suzanne?

Instead I am a stranger when I visit France, a delighted spectator, gratefully learning to abide. I am not a Frenchman, but we have a small French house to go to. We savor the trees and hills around Puivert, the glorious fields and woods where animals and birds reside, and the village itself. Painters refer to the human figures they add as a last touch to their landscapes as "staffage"—and so Suzanne and I are staffage in our beloved French place and American home. The first few times we went to Puivert, early in our visits, I felt lonely and alienated, especially as darkness was coming on in the evenings and we were preparing for bed. Mornings were better than the sad twilight feeling. I have grown more used to being in France, but still it is not our home.

Wisconsin is our home now, but in Soldiers Grove we are also curiosities. Our neighbors are polite but don't know what to make of us—this aging couple who came to the area only a few years ago, living on a ridge top with a garage full of books, playing strange music, roaming the fields and woods in all weather, spending hours and hours scribbling at desks, reading ponderous two-day-old Eastern newspapers, and abandoning their place for months every year to go to Europe. When we speak to our neighbors our talk is of weather or crops, perhaps spiced with some local gossip. The conversations are brief, and sometimes we go for weeks without speaking to anyone. Is this home?

But what is "home"? Maybe it is the light warmth coming off the skin, perhaps the pale light that the body gives off. Perhaps our home now is nature—trees, sky, pastures, valleys, and hills—American and French. Can we be at home in places where we have not lived the customs, places we can't remember before they existed in our minds, where we do not know how to communicate with our neighbors?

We moved frequently in our lives to opportunities, abandoning homes, leaving friends behind, and this is what we have come to: our tidy home at the end of a two-mile dirt road near Soldiers Grove, Wisconsin, where we live among work and traditions not our own; and a place in France, an ancient house in Puivert, where we cannot speak the language. So we will conclude our lives as strangers. Does age make outsiders of us? Perhaps we all inevitably become strangers in the end.

We stand on the third-floor terrace in Puivert at dawn as mist washes over the slopes, picking up the rising sunlight from the east—subtle pinks and blues, a pastel chrome brightness hovering around the staunch silhouette of the foothills. It fades quickly, and the change is rapid. The light becomes more defined, less lyrical, mostly silver and gray and light cream as the morning begins. Wagtails scramble on the red roof tiles across the lane. The rooster in the garden behind the house gives us his full repertoire—caw and variations—then grows silent. In the distance a dog barks at a rabbit in the bush.

We look out from our home in Soldiers Grove. The Kickapoo valley is full of morning fog, like a ghostly lake; we watch the mist break and slip up the hillside, snagging through the trees. A grouse drums on the next ridge, and horned larks swing over the field stubble, going *tsee, tsee,* squeeking to draw attention away from their nests in the grass. In the bottom of the south ridge at the edge of woods, three deer gaze and listen as they munch. Suddenly they bound away into the trees, their white tails wagging through the underbrush. We finish our tea, put on jackets, and stroll out to become staffage in these morning hues.

Every day at some point I think of France and the little house in Puivert—our root place to which we migrate each year like bobolinks to Argentina. But this book is mostly about home, our house, woods, and fields near Soldiers Grove, Wisconsin, with some memories along the way of how, at last, we came to be strangers in these friendly places.

Trees

Of our 117 acres near Soldiers Grove, 43 have been cleared
on the ridge top for hay and pasturing. The rest are heavily
wooded acres down the slopes of the ridges. This is typical of
the area. It is lovely to gaze down on the canopies of the trees.
When you drive through this countryside in warm weather it
is verdant. There are small dairy and hay farms on the ridge
tops and strung through the valleys, some more than a century
old. The working life is difficult and the economy is tight. Too
many places are abandoned or lost. Young people are moving
away, but we are glad to be living in the trees.

Over the more than forty years of our marriage, Suzanne
and I have owned five houses. I always took great pleasure in
the trees that were on our lots in the towns. Somehow it made
me feel significant that we "owned" them. I cherished them,
occasionally trimmed and watered them, and spent a lot of
time regarding and enjoying their changes. Now for the rest of
our lives we will live with countless trees sweeping down the
sides of our ridge, and through the draws and notches between
the slopes. They no longer make me feel significant, and with
some difficulty I have learned that I do not own them.

At first I thought I would try to be a good yeoman and keep
my woods clean and trim as a park. I was quickly discouraged

in this endeavor. I lacked time, expertise, equipment, and energy. When I finally realized that the best I could do would be to maintain a few paths and clear some of the downed trees for firewood, I relaxed in the presence of the woods. I had worked hard at jobs for forty-five years, but the trees were not going to be my new job. They were not even my "responsibility," beyond making sure I did not burn them down. The trees precede me and will survive me. They do not exist for my edification, nor do I exist for theirs. They are my privilege, but I am not a privilege to them. I am a much happier person now that I have finally come to this conclusion. Oak, hickory, elm, maple, poplar, birch, aspen, wild cherry, cedar, spruce, and black walnut. I am content simply to live quietly for a brief while among them.

But I came to this happy conclusion the hard way. Eino Paasikivi left a chain saw, several axes, a hatchet, wedges, and some splitting mauls. On our early rambles in the woods we noticed that a large red oak had fallen deep among the trees on the north slope. It was a big, venerable tree, probably a hundred years old. Carpenter ants had wounded it and a big wind finally blew it over. It had shivered saplings and bowed resilient birch trees when it fell. There was sadness in the place where it had fallen, as if some wisdom had been violated.

But it represented a large supply of firewood, so I trimmed a path to it through the woods and backed the old Ford tractor down until I could reach the tree with a long chain. Then I cut a large section from the trunk and hooked on. I felt very rustic and robust as I did this work, clanging the tools around and revving the tractor. But I hung the tractor up on an old stump in the mud and when I finally got it off—as they say in our area—I "buried it" in soft earth. I unhooked and spent some time shoveling under the wheels and pulling the tractor out with our four-wheel-drive pickup. Then I cautiously backed the truck in as far as I dared, sawed the oak up into toteable sections, and lugged some of them uphill to the truck bed. When I finally got a load out of the woods and up beside the Morton building, I was exhausted but pleased with myself that I had at least accomplished this much.

Of course I should have quit for the day, but the work ethic prevailed. I began slicing the logs into sections narrow enough to split. The sound of a chain saw is a raw, loveless noise; it bites into a morning or an afternoon, and the uproar exhausts you. The big McCullough worked well, but the logs were thicker than the bar, so they had to be horsed over as I worked, then I had to roll the saw to meet my cut. It was difficult work and, in my inexperience and exhaustion, I did it awkwardly, making it even more tiring.

Finally I finished the sectioning, but instead of going into the house to rest like a sensible, experienced swain, I began working with the axes and maul to begin the splitting. Cutting and splitting firewood is rewarding but mindless, archetypal work. I love the smell of wood as it opens. Someone once told me that firewood heats you at least five times: when you cut it, when you haul it, when you split it, when you stack it, and when you burn it. But the work is hard, especially for someone who has spent most of his adult life sitting at a desk. I have asthma and was pumping hard. Sweat chilled my skin and my stomach burned. At least I had the wits to sit down and rest frequently. But I was *managing* our woods; there were no excuses. As I flailed with the maul, wind blew the red baseball hat from my head. When I finally caught up with it, I stood in the chill dusk, breathing hard, realizing I had been given a sign. I put the tools away and lurched to the house. Fortunately I had not done serious injury to myself. But in my weariness over the next few days I began rethinking my work methods and my attitude toward the trees.

It took another episode to bring me fully to wisdom. The view from our house and deck into the valley is dazzling.

Paasikivi did a good job of keeping the woods trimmed back, but toward the end of his time he had become ill and could not keep up. Several smaller trees were intruding into our vista, and I determined to take them down. I don't relish cutting down live trees, especially when they grow on hillsides. When they are on a slope it is difficult to tell which way they are leaning. I dropped several without incident. I was weary by the time I got to the largest one, a poplar that had grown quite tall among its competitors. It would have been a good time to quit.

I circled it, sizing it up, notched it "by the book," and began slicing toward the notch from the other side. I have heard that a person cut suddenly by a knife doesn't instantly feel the wound; it takes a moment for the body to realize it has been rendered. I imagined that the tree, having established itself on the hillside for several years, didn't "realize" what was happening. It held in silence over my head as I cut, then almost as if it suddenly perceived its wound, it pinched down on the saw bar and shut the chain down. The tree and I stood together in the quiet for minute—victim and assassin. A slight breeze sighed for the last time high in its canopy. I let go of the saw handle and wiped my forehead.

I was exhausted and vacuous, irritated that I had been hung up. I didn't have the presence of mind to realize that the tree could have rolled off its stump and killed or maimed me at that moment. Thank God it was not my adversary. Instead, slowly, with resignation, before I knew what was happening, it tilted and began arcing down through the saplings to crash heavily into the sod. It lay vulnerable and somber in the rising dust and broken underbrush. I thought I heard its last gasps. I felt like a brute. Once again, I hauled the tools up the hill and put them away.

Suzanne hadn't wanted me to drop the trees. When I went into the house she asked how it had gone. I was ashamed and

could not tell her. I went off to brood. In my weariness I rumi-
nated again about trees, slowly beginning to recognize my
place with them.

My plan to clear the brush from between the trees in some
areas became victim of reality, so prickly ash and berry bushes
sometimes scourge us when we tour the woods. But tranquility
is our reward—and silence. There is only birdsong, insect
drone, breezes, the occasional distant sigh of a pickup on a
county road, or the light bourdon of a high jet on its way to
Chicago or Minneapolis. In hot weather when we move under
their canopies, the trees gently spray and cool us. We are always
surprised by the silence; it enters our minds in all seasons.

Not only do trees give us peace, they give us succor. When
Suzanne and I ramble down the sides of our ridges to explore
old fence lines, our ascent back up is steep and strenuous. We
give ourselves a purchase by pulling up on small trees and
saplings. If we stop for a rest in the woods I find a smaller,
pliant tree, a birch if I can locate one, and lean back against it,
bone on wood, to let the suppleness of the tree ease the tired-
ness in my aging back.

There is sharp division between seasons on this Upper Midwestern landscape. I always look forward to the changes. When
I was a very young bard years ago, I heard Theodore Roethke
read his poems and he commented that "a poet needs to feel a
bit of the heat, and a bit of the cold."

In winter, when leaves are down, it is an abiding pleasure to
look deep into the woods. The trees seem more stately and
defined in their manifest suspension than in summer when
they blend into each other and the green underbrush. New
things are revealed to us, stands of undiscovered trees and hol-
lowed-out places in crotches or at the base of large trees where
animals reside. I had never realized how extensive some of

these chambers are, providing continuous housing in venerable trees for raccoons, skunks, owls, foxes, and birds.

We find old apple trees tucked into the edges of our woods, a few of them still healthy and abundant. When we come across them, we always discuss how we will care for them, clear brush and vines away to give them breathing room. But there are a dozen full-time commercial orchards in our area and, beginning in late summer, fine apples are abundant. Still we romance about our fruits, always picking a few of the least spotted ones to munch on as we walk. We also nibble the bearings of our wild plum and mulberry trees.

Elms are graceful, tragic trees. They begin bravely as saplings leaning out over the fields. But they are already wounded and bleeding within, attacked by the fungus elm disease. For a while they seem to thrive, but then begin struggling to maintain their foliage, rarely making it beyond ten years. When they die they turn gray and are like clusters of ghosts along the edges of meadows. Although their grain is twisted and difficult to split, the dead trees make good firewood, so I take as many as I can, but I can't keep up. When I saw down the deadwood, they have a blood-red ring, which shows when they were first assaulted by the contagion. Beside my writing shack there is an unusually large elm standing in the open where it has not been closely exposed to afflicted trees. It has grown tall and its canopy spreads out in a distinctive shape that can be seen even from the distant road that runs between Soldiers Grove and Gays Mills. It marks our place. Late last summer its leaves browned suddenly and were blown away by high winds. I thought it was the end, but this spring it rallied and has greened forth handsomely again. I celebrated by wiring a bluebird house to its trunk.

We discovered old farm roads down each side of our ridge, mostly overgrown, but still traceable through the trees. We assume these were the entrance roads to the old farm Paasikivi obliterated. These old cart paths were used before the gravel road was brought in by the township over the ridge top. We have cleared the north road so that it is now a pleasant walk down the slope. We thought about clearing the south road as well but decided to leave it overgrown, as it comes out close to River Road and we do not invite interruption of our solitude. We leave the trees and bushes to protect our silence.

Sky

SOMETIMES UP ON THE RIDGE it feels like we have two-thirds sky in our prospect. It is a prominent part of our lives. We have lived mostly in cities and towns, and it is constant wonderment for us to step outside and behold the uninhibited sweep of daylight or dark.

Some mornings the sun rises through a cream of mist like an egg yolk or some marvelous confection. On clear dawns it bulges out of the horizon as a fiery mushroom. Clouds are various, ebullient, and full of moods. Sometimes they are ridged magnificently like surf rolling up from the horizon. Or they can be soft petals, the whole sky filled with them, as if we are living under a pond full of lily pads. There are great days of looming alabaster towers, an architect's most extravagant dreams, unfastening, softly turning, and cohering massively in the azure.

Some weeks, day after day, the clouds are unmoving, an impenetrable shroud over our heads. We yearn for relief, a small tear in the heavy curtain, an easement of bright light that will give us some energy to go on. Other days they roll hell-bent over our heads for endless hours, volitant curtains spraying down chill rain or snow. There are winter days that begin bright, then small bundles of clouds cohere and thicken;

eventually snow feathers down, the showers thicken, the trees
and fields disappear. It snows and snows.

I am born of a family with slight curvature of the spine.
All of us walk slightly bent over. As I grow older, increasingly
I shuffle bent with my eyes on the ground. But on the ridge I
compel myself to unbend and look up. It's like keeping your
eye on the ball. Otherwise you miss the marvelous passage and
action of clouds and stars, the great show you ignore when you
have to live in town.

I remember a twilight when the sun descended into a bundle of storm clouds in the west, casting red-orange stripes
against the deepening purple. Another day there was a covering of clouds stretching out, but leaving the whole horizon
open. The settling light slipped over the top of this lid, making
it glow underneath, then brushed the tall billow cumulus
clouds soaring in the open east with a glowing orange. The
sun slipped down farther and the light became pink in a band
along the horizon, highlighting barns, silos, houses, and woods.
Finally, almost as an encore, there was an opening, and the
three-quarter moon shone through the billows. This display
went on for twenty minutes and we were transfixed, viewing it
from a bench along the road. When it was over we rose to our
feet and applauded.

Some nights I step out on the deck to look at the night sky
before going to bed. The moon dominates when it is out, full
or partial, meandering and fickle, slipping up and going down
when you least expect it. Juliet begs Romeo not to swear by the
"inconstant moon, / That monthly changes in her circled orb, /
Lest that thy love prove likewise variable." One clear night it
was full with a broad, brilliant ring extending far out, composed of ice crystals, rounding through most of the sky. It was
like a slightly soiled softball flung high above the field lights by
a canny pitcher—illusive and unpredictable. When there are
thin clouds the moon dusts them with light, creating at times a

halo so bright the aura casts my night shadow across the
boards of the deck. The moon, moving behind the scales of a
mackerel sky, is like the eye of a hungry fish. Seven hundred
years ago the anonymous Scottish poet of "Sir Patrick Spens"
wrote: "Late, late yestreen I saw the new moone / wi' the auld
moone in hir arme." No poet has ever improved on this.

In a poem I made about being in the country after a long
period of living in a city I wrote, "How could I have forgotten
all these stars?" Now on every clear night they are mine to
glory in. I will never forget them again. Even to my aging eyes,
the lights continue to multiply the longer I stay out in the dark,
the brilliant scattered dust and the familiar configurations.
Through all this the stripe of the Milky Way dominates; in
summer it glisters across our gravel road and in winter it runs
along the length of it.

My neighbor Richie Halverson says, "You don't forget the
stars. I've lived here all my life. I'm in the milking shed at
night. Then I'm tired, walk right in to supper, watch a little
television, and fall into bed. But sometimes I still stop and take
a look on my way in. I think about when I was a kid lying out
on the hay bales. Stars can still surprise you."

The sky can bring big trouble, too. Heavy clouds suddenly
appear and rush in before I can hustle to shelter or cover my
head. They carry heavy rain or snows. A few years ago I was
mowing the yard and wearing ear guards. I glanced up to see
evil-looking blackness charging in overhead. I couldn't get the
mower under cover in time, so I abandoned it. By the time I
made it to the house and shut a few windows, heavy rain was
horizontal, slamming up against the side of the house. Lightning
was continuous, the house trembled, wind shrieked through
the gutters, terrifying our dog. There was a greenish-yellow
light. We decided to shut ourselves into the inner bathroom
and wait it out. The power went out as we cowered, pitching us
into darkness. The storm passed in twenty minutes, but when

we emerged and went outside, there were limbs down everywhere. It was still gray and the landscape looked chastened. We
walked into the woods and saw that big trees had been toppled.

The phone was dead so we drove out the gravel road to see
how our neighbors had fared. Richie Halverson's tobacco shed
was flattened. He and his wife had been in their barn when it
hit. Richie said he felt "mortal" as the building wavered and
shook around them. The roof from his shed flew off and clob-
bered four cows. They were lying bloody in the field and he
was probably going to lose them. Jake Yant lost big trees, and
sheets of siding were ripped from his house. He pointed out a
path of broken branches and trees through the woods where it
seemed like a small whirlwind had smashed through.

Tornadoes are always a concern in our area, and people are
spellbound as well as threatened by them. My daughter, Justine,
is a metalsmith and sculptor, living in Iowa. A recurring theme
in her work is large and small renderings of tornadoes, which
she skillfully forms with wire or cable. They are vivid objects,
embodying great power and energy. Some of her commis-
sioned civic pieces are over twenty feet tall, and others are tiny
vortexes of just a few inches. Midwesterners cluster around
them in fascination when she shows her work.

But mostly there are miracles and delights in the sky. Walking out one night, we noticed a flickering in the north. It was
aurora borealis—the fourth time in my life I have been blessed
by this glory, and this was a full-fledged display. We watched
the arcane, flickering lights, the sudden glimmerings, the huge
fingers of purple, pink, and rose light rolling and flashing over
each other. They weren't just bouncing on the horizon, but
were streaking brilliantly out to the center of the sky. We saw
another phenomenon I had never witnessed before: patches of
rose-colored light in some areas of the aurora, perhaps the
reflection of sunset, but a florid vision, a feast of astonishment

to the eye. We were not sitting on a bench for this show, but remained on our feet in awe.

Then there was 1997 and the summer of the comet. It was like a bonus to our lives. We had looked forward to Comet Haley in 1986, but it had been a disappointment. We were living in town and never even got a glimpse of it. We had resigned ourselves to never seeing a comet. We read about Comet Hale-Bopp in the newspaper but figured it would just be another bust. Then we walked out one Wisconsin night and a ball of radiance came over like a streamlined train crossing above the continent, serenely passing over our gravel road, riding through the broad stripe of our galaxy, leaving a sheen of shifting colors in its wake as it diminished each evening. On any clear night we went out to watch the comet. By autumn it was gone, its absence creating a great void. We had grown used to it, and now the sky seemed incomplete without its magnificent nightly passage.

Poetry

Poetry completes my life; it is a verity for all my days. I began wanting to be a poet after I was drafted into the army in the mid-1950s. Frightened, lonely, and bored by mindlessness, I discovered that I like to read. At first it was fiction and popular history, but then I found poetry. I was fascinated by how poets use words. Sometimes the words were obscure, but always sensitive, intelligent, and challenging, far more impressive than the words of journalists, politicians, or glib popular writers.

Eventually I began scribbling my own verse and kept it on soiled papers in my shirt pocket, slipping off to the edge of the platoon during smoke breaks to write on my little sheets. If anyone asked what I was doing, I said I was writing a letter to my girlfriend. In fact, if I showed my poems to anyone, it was to girls. Usually they thought I was strange, but sometimes they were impressed.

I tried to imitate the masters I read in the anthologies. It was the start of my long practice, and I began to recognize the challenges and possibilities of poetry. When I got out of the army and finished lurching through the rest of my undergraduate college years, there were no writing programs or seminars available to me, so I struck out on my own. Somehow I had the sense to realize that choosing to become a poet is a serious business, a life decision, but I never looked back.

Since then, through my adult life, I have spent a lot of time and thought looking for places to *be* a poet. America doesn't pay its poets by the hour, nor does it provide them with tax-free villas. To sustain my precious habit, I needed to find a way to make my living. Fortunately, my jobs were interesting and reasonably supportive. Until we had children, I wrote in the evenings after supper, and for decades I closed my office door on lunch hours to work at poems. When the children grew older, I arose early in the mornings and wrote at home before going to my job. On weekends I toiled at small tables tucked away in far-flung corners of our various houses.

I am always grateful to be able to work at poems; it is a process that brings my life full circle. But time and space have always been a problem, and for years I dreamed of perfect conditions. I read accounts of poets' outposts with unrelenting envy: Wordsworth's Dove Cottage, Robinson Jeffers's Tor House, the Brownings' villa in Italy, Ezra Pound's retreat in Rapallo, Robert Frost's cottage at Ripton, Donald Hall's farm in New Hampshire, Mark Van Doren's place in Cornwall, Connecticut, and, yes, Thoreau's Walden. Once I met Archibald MacLeish and he gave me happy accounts of his Conway, Massachusetts, farm. How did these poets come to have such tranquil, prolific environs?

I suppressed my yearnings. We had no family legacies and my jobs provided a living income, but nothing extra. Eventually, by teaching on the side for a couple of years and saving money from poetry readings, I managed to scrape up enough money to purchase a small cabin in the woods and farmland of northwestern Pennsylvania. It was a two-and-a-half-hour drive from Pittsburgh, but almost every Friday afternoon, late after work, we'd throw things into our Volkswagen van, round up the kids and dogs, and head for the country until Sunday afternoon, when we'd take the whole show back to Pittsburgh again. Despite limitations of time and space, all of us acquired our taste for the woods and countryside on these blessed outings.

Back of the cabin there was an old toolshed, which I cleaned out, insulated, and made into a writing place. I stuffed myself into it every weekend morning—just room for a chair and a small board up on two-by-fours—and happily worked at poems. But eventually we moved away from Pennsylvania and had to sell the cabin. I felt like Judas, as if I had bartered my soul. For ten years it had been my psychic home and now I was betraying it. It was the beginning of great longing, an extended desire to refill this void I had created.

For years I worked in university towns and had no situation for retreat. A friend invited us to visit his country house in the north Georgia mountains and was astonished to find that I did not even own a pair of jeans or walking shoes. "Zimmer," he told me, "you need some real pants." We moved to Iowa and my yearning did not cease. I devoted what spare moments I had to poems. Eventually we decided to mount a search for a modest place in the country, and southwestern Wisconsin fell into the circle of possibilities.

I recall reading an account of Carl Sandburg when, after a long search, he finally found the place he dreamed of in the glorious Carolina hill country. He turned to his wife and said in exultation, "This is the place," and she agreed. I said the same thing to Suzanne when we first drove out on the ridge in the driftless hills. We looked into the valley together and held hands. Already both of us had begun to scheme how we would gather our modest resources.

We had separate visions for ourselves and for each other. Suzanne has studied political and social development all her life. She wanted the farm not only because it is beautiful, but also for complex reasons having to do with independence and self-reliance. Both of us wanted a pleasurable place for our-selves, and for our children and grandchildren, a renewal of the delight and peace we had all shared in the northern Penn-sylvania countryside. But I wanted it for poetry most of all.

I wanted solitude, the stimulation and reprise of nature, a place where I could explore all the possibilities of my poems without having to feel the pressures of other work, where I would have uninhibited hours for writing.

I had a shack—ten by twelve feet, about the size of Walden—built and placed it on a rise just where the road curves gracefully toward the house. There are windows looking into woods on one side and the valley on the other. A few pic-tures hang on the wall: W. B. Yeats, Charlie Parker, Roberto Clemente, Mary Lou Williams, Fritzie Zivic, John Clare, the Brontë sisters. But it is very spare, a place for words. My name, Zimmer, means "room" in German. So I have a quiet *zimmer* to slip away to, a place where I engage the holy words.

Neighbors

THERE IS A DIFFERENCE between neighboring in town and in the country. In the university towns where we lived for thirty years, people in neighborhoods dwelled together and yet very much apart. Invisible dividing lines were rarely crossed; people made a few allowances, gave a little space, but mostly ignored each other. Although our houses and property lines were only some yards apart, the distances were enormous. For instance, on our street in Iowa City there were full professors, low professors, high townies, low townies, doctors, dentists, high administrators, low administrators, and even a few graduate students living in bungalows owned by high townies or full professors. The size of the house was relative to the resident's high or low stature. Interaction was rare and usually accidental. People stayed in their houses and yards, went about their business cognizant of their places, guarding their positions and privacy.

Along our block there were three large doctors' houses in a row, then our modest residence at the end. One of the doctors had a driving snowblower and on nasty winter mornings he liked to get out early to clear the sidewalks of the other doctors, doing them a favor, going almost the length of the block, but stopping and turning around exactly where our sidewalk began.

We learned to avoid our neighbors, speaking only when we happened upon them. They were unaware of our triumphs and difficulties, and we became easily content to let them do their own living and coping. When I was a child in Ohio, neighborhoods were welcoming places; people shared birthdays, holidays, good soup, war news, bad and good health news, cakes and pies. They even gave each other permanents. But when we moved into our house in Iowa City near the university, no one greeted us or brought over a pie—and no one stopped in to say good-bye when we left a dozen years later.

I was moving some chairs into our country house on our first day in the driftless hills when Richie Halverson drove up on his motor scooter, a weed cutter in his hand. He said he'd been out checking his hay and thought he would just stop over to introduce himself. He offered to help me carry in the chairs. He is an engaging, articulate, gray-blond man, his face and arms rugged and worn from years in the sun and fields. Eino Paasikivi had told me that Richie rented the fields from him in summer and harvested the hay. I didn't wait for Richie to ask, but told him we would be pleased if he continued to do this. Of course, we knew nothing of field care and husbandry, and we were anxious about our new obligations to the land.

We offered coffee, and Richie talked for a long while. His family has been farming the area for a hundred years. His pretty century farm is on County Highway C, two miles down our dirt road, then a quarter mile out on the highway. When we walk to the top of our ridge we can see his white farmhouse and barns in the distance. Richie's talk is rambling. He spoke, in no particular order, of fields, cows, children, barns, tractors, milking equipment, rainfall, sunshine, deer, baseball, coyotes, turkeys, corn, oats, horses, timothy, and alfalfa. When he got up to leave he asked if there was any way he and his family might help us. He told us to call him if we had any problems.

He offered to look in on our place when we were gone during the week. He was glad we had taken it and was sure we would enjoy being in the country. He wanted us to stop by his farm and meet his wife and children; he would show us his cows and milking operation. Late in the afternoon his daughter delivered an apple pie Mrs. Halverson had baked.

The only time he showed reserve was when I asked him about our nearest neighbor, who lives a mile back down the dirt road along the ridge top. I sensed bad blood immediately, but Richie was reserved in his comments. I had seen the name Yant on the mailbox. Eino Paasikivi had told me of trouble with one of his neighbors, mostly over roving cows and boundary-line squabbles. I figured Jake Yant was the adversary, and perhaps a difficult person, while noting, too, that Eino was a very stubborn and proud man.

Later in the day Will Cobble, our neighbor at the bottom of our steep ridge of trees on Highway C, drove up in his pickup to greet us. He is not a farmer, but is married to Richie Halverson's sister. He has a supervisory job with the county highway department and his family has also lived in the area for many years. Paasikivi had set a standard for solitude on our ridge and Will continues to respect it with us. We rarely see him, although he, too, offered his help if we ever have the need.

We looked for Jake Yant when we drove out the road on errands. He and his wife have a handsome spread over the same ridge we live on, and they maintain a herd of beef cattle in their fields. We pieced together bits and pieces from comments made by Richie Halverson and Will Cobble about ongoing arguments over hunting territory, old dried bad blood about land use and ownership, and enduring bitterness about ugly things said in the midst of squabbles—but we bore in mind that there are two sides to every quarrel.

Richie told me one bizarre and absurdly funny story. Richie's talk is sometimes discursive, but he drives his narratives like poems: "Yant and Eino got into it hot and heavy one day about something, and Yant finally tells Eino he don't have access through his field roads no more. This means Eino can't go across Yant's land to get to his double pastures, and that's the only level way in. That's hard on Eino, but he's damned if he'll beg. So he hires a young guy named Digger Doug, who is working cheap to get started in the excavation business, and has him run his bulldozer down a grade and up through some woods on his property so's he can get to his fields. Trouble is, the new road starts to wash when it rains and it's going to erode. So Eino brings Digger back and has him make a big run with his oil truck down one hill and up the other, spilling road oil on the cut they made. Then he brings a load of crush in his dump and runs down the hill okay with it. But when he gets halfway up the other hill he gets stuck. They phone me up and I bring my heavy tractor over to pull him out. They don't know what the hell they're gonna do. The only way they can get the job done is to come across Yant's field road, but Eino would rather eat little balls of turkey shit than ask permission. So Eino talks Digger into making a sneak attack. They come in after dark with the load and Digger turns off his truck lights. They peek in Yant's window and make sure he is watching tele-vision, then ease it down the gravel road. Eino gets out and takes off the chain across the entrance to Yant's field road. They run the truck real slow and quiet across Yant's property to Eino's pastures. Then they creep back out, put the chain back on, and go off for a beer. In the morning Digger revs it up and comes flying down the grade, and spreads the load of rocks and crush on the upgrade. Somehow he gets it down pretty even and gets back up the hill. Yant never knew how they got it done. That was twenty years ago and that road is still in pretty good shape."

Yant did not make an appearance at our house and we had no occasion to speak to him. He probably thought I had been put off by Eino's and Richie's stories. We finally left a note in his mailbox and he called. We invited him and his wife to stop by for an afternoon tea. They were pleasant and guarded. He made a few passing remarks about locals to test our attitude, but he was mostly judicious and engaging, and he displayed a good sense of humor. People in town complain about him and his methods. Someone quietly advised me not to refer to him as my neighbor, but to just say that I live near him.

Yant and I arranged to meet and congenially walked our boundaries together. I decided to put it on the line: I wanted to write, garden, read, take walks, and be quiet on my land, and I knew he was busy with his own operations. I suggested that we do whatever fencing and adjustment was necessary to stay out of each other's hair. He seemed impressed by my straightforwardness. We shook hands.

When we drive past his place and see him in his yard or out walking we stop for a chat. We do not discuss politics, local business, or social issues. He has good knowledge and appreciation of the plant and animal life in the area, and we ask him questions. We are friendly and have a workable arrangement—and we have stayed out of each other's hair.

Birds

In all seasons our breezy ridge top is a table and launching pad into the valley for birds. Smaller birds come to our feeders, then wing out, dipping, pumping and rising, dipping again, pumping and rising. But larger birds shoot out in a straight line with all their power. Only the mightiest winds deter or make the crows and hawks waver. We see crows flapping strongly in high winds over the point of our ridge, making no progress at all for minutes at a time, apparently enjoying the challenge and exercise.

Bird species come and go and populations shift. In their seasons, we see swallows in the evenings; bobolinks when the grass is tall; horned larks after hay has been taken; orioles in autumn; chickadees, buntings, robins, thrashers, finches, wrens, titmice, nuthatches, hummingbirds, bluebirds, flickers, cedar waxwings, cardinals, blue jays, red-winged blackbirds, warblers, doves, quail, grouse, geese, bobwhites, grosbeaks, pheasants, woodpeckers pileated and redheaded, turkey buzzards, wild turkeys in big nervous flocks pecking in the fields; hawks, usually in pairs diving and soaring; a splendid pair of northern harriers; and occasionally even bald eagles in from the Mississippi. Other birds stop briefly on their journeys and we do not even have time to identify them. We occasionally hear our resident owl at night but have seen it only once. Sandhill cranes live in the marsh along the river in the valley, and we watch their solemn bobbing and turning rituals through our field glasses like voyeurs.

We choose to feed the birds that stay through winter. In those difficult months we keep two feeders supplied. One of them hangs above the deck overlooking the valley. The other is a flat board, like an aircraft carrier mounted on a two-by-four in the snowy yard where birds swoop in to feed in turns of species and sexes. They scutter, raid, and run each other off in great swirls. Every morning on my way to my writing shack, I stop to sweep snow from the board and give them millet, thistles, cracked corn, and sunflower seeds.

In summer, birds that nest on the ground must be particularly resilient, especially in the hay fields. Loss and disappointment are almost continuous. Larger birds ravage their nests in the grass. Richie Halverson has taken the hay twice each summer, and turkeys, bobolinks, and larks never seem to complete their nesting before he wrecks them with his big cutter bar. We are "setting aside" our fields next year with the Department of Natural Resources to avoid these disasters, joining a ten-year program in which we agree not to harvest our fields.

Bobolinks are great tragic actors. They perch on milkweed stalks and scream at us, or fall in the roadside ahead as we walk, chattering, faking terrible injuries, hopping and fluttering along, trying to divert our attention from the eggs in their nests. Swallows dive at us and feign attacks, swoop down, coming almost within arm's reach. We see groups of small birds running off large birds and hawks, thrusting and pecking at them, alas, probably after their nests have already been violated. Their bravery always amazes us.

We were walking the field road up the hill to the double meadows on the north ridge when a small bundle of fluffed brown feathers came shrieking out of the underbrush to peck at Suzanne's boot. It was a mother grouse protecting her brood. Suzanne retreated, but the little bird followed her and continued its attack. She was so vehement that we hurried on up the road, much to the hawing amusement of two crows perched in a dead elm branch over our heads. One of them plopped some white mucilage on my shoulder as I hustled up the hill, making me feel very much like the silly, gasping interloper I was.

In rainy seasons the Kickapoo sometimes overflows its loops and the river runs into the fields. Then water birds come in from the Mississippi ten miles away—egrets stretching their long bodies as they fold and unfold their elegant wings; sandhill cranes spiraling, rasping, and cautioning each other; and even swans in heavy, swooping lines to feed on grain in the swampy fields.

Richie Halverson tells this story: "A flock of swans come in from the river and got into my corn. I went out there and those guys were really tucking it in. I got mad and wasn't thinking much, so I got my shotgun and gave them both barrels. They took off, but I noticed one flopped down in the corn and hid quiet. I figured it had taken some pellets, and I was wondering whether swan meat would make a good dinner. I walked into the corn and seen him out of the corner of my eye pressed down in the stalks. He must have been an old guy. The younger ones are kind of brown, but he was pure white and his feathers was frazzled. I put my gun down and made a dive for him. He starts to make a crazy noise like one of them toy horns that kids have. My God! That bird like to beat my head off! Them wings is strong! It slapped me on my ears and knocked my glasses off, kept punching till I let go. Then it run off. My head was ringing and my nose was bleeding. I felt like I'd been in there with Tyson. I couldn't find my glasses, finally had to throw my hat down for a marker, and went to fetch Nora to help me. She had a good laugh; told me swan meat ain't fit for alligators. Then she got a little sad. She told me that swans mate for life and the other one was probably around somewhere. But we never seen 'em again. By the time we found my glasses the whole day was shot and it was time for milking."

In late summer and early autumn we hear raucous noise and look up to see great wobbling V's of geese beating the air as they head south. At times there are over a hundred, exhorting each other and undulating in wind curtains. We watch them disappear over the distant ridges and resign ourselves to the changes that are coming. Once, as we watched a passage, two birds seemed to interact on the right wing of the formation, fussing at each other and making extracurricular runs. Then the whole flock got out of whack, scrambled, honking mightily, came together again in some disarray before reassembling the V to continue south. It seemed as if there had been a dispute over the arrangement of the formation and things had to be settled quickly so the group could proceed. We marveled at their efficiency.

We often surprise large broods of wild turkeys when we take our walks. We are never able to get close, but see them scurrying off in the distant fields—mama, papa, and usually at least a dozen youngsters, fanning out into the underbrush. If they are really startled, they take long runs in the fields like jetliners, then launch themselves into heavy, swooping flights to land swinging in treetop branches. If we are able to catch them unaware, we watch from a distance and see the pompous displays of the male, opening his fan and strutting for the females, reminding the flock and all potential rivals that he is boss turkey. The females are smaller and more sensible, foraging on their own or in small groups, revolving their heads in every direction like periscopes as they feed. They seem so vulnerable in the open fields, but their acute sight and hearing afford them marvelous protection. We rarely see one closer than a hundred yards, except for those that are shot by hunters. When Richie Halverson runs into their nests with his mower the mother sometimes bravely holds her place, covering the eggs, and is destroyed by the blades. Crows and turkey buzzards come to haul out the remains, and we find only bloody feathers and bits of shell.

We rarely find bird plumage on our walks—sometimes a few turkey feathers or the black slash of a crow feather in the grass. Because of their brightness, we occasionally find cardinal or blue jay plumes, but so far no sky-blue bunting feathers. On a field road through the woods we found elegant black feathers with round white spots on them. I showed them to neighbors and they had never seen anything quite like them. Finally, after consulting many bird books, we decided they were from a downy woodpecker. They are such reclusive birds; it surprised us to find their feathers in such a well-traveled place. Perhaps a hawk or owl had knocked it down into the road.

Early one February as we trudged through heavy snow, we heard an unusual sound from the south woods, like someone beating the inside of a bucket with a wooden spoon. Suzanne figured it was a grouse drumming. Usually this is spring activity, but he was banging away in midwinter—a grand, big rat-a-tat-tat for such a little bird. Obviously he was slightly confused, as there would hardly be any females swooning to his drumming in this frigid weather. Probably he was an old grouse, a little muddled, like an aging man wishing for love in a preposterous season.

We have many migrating bird visitors between seasons, and their comings and goings are only hints of vast, formidable movements. On a rainy day a huge mixed flock of grackles, cowbirds, and starlings swooped in and completely covered the grassy point at the end of our ridge. They spread out, pecking for worms and insects. They all seemed to know their place

and which ten square inches were theirs to browse. Considering
what big, tough birds they are, it surprised me that there was
so little fussing, but they were en route to Mexico and coopera-
tion was essential. They lingered for perhaps ten minutes,
pecking, moving quietly, then suddenly, on some signal, swirled
up in a great, twisting dark cloud and were gone. There were
hundreds of them, maybe a thousand. Migration is a kind of
history, marking the annals. These movements always seem
very significant to me, a kind of avian chronicle that measures
the years.

And history in this area is as difficult to trace as migration.
Because old-timers have been talking to each other for years,
they leave out assumed details of time and space when I press
them for stories. I might be told that a great blizzard lasted
three days, people lost their lives, some were pinned in their
farms for many days before relief came, their cows freezing in
the pastures—but the year of this tragedy is not revealed. It
might have been five years ago or fifty. Nor am I given details
about temperature, snow depth, endurance, and recovery.

   Richie Halverson tells me he thinks he might have seen a
wolf on our land, but he doesn't say whether it was last week
or twenty years ago. Then he'll remember quick, tantalizing
snippets of stories about old days when there were bears in
these hills and even some mountain lions. I can't tell whether
he is telling me his own stories, his father's, or his grandfather's. Then, before I can press him for details, he'll switch to
telling me how he is having trouble with mold in his corn
crop, then goes on to discuss the current baseball standings.
Richie rambles. His talk is full of surprises, he makes odd con-
nections, and his narratives unfold with tension and lyricism.
I am not the only poet in the driftless hills.

Making Poetry

Camerado, this is no book,
Who touches this touches a man.

Walt Whitman

Here is another small history. As a young man I worked on my poems weekends and vacations, on time off from my jobs, and I wanted to be a poet *all* the time. After some years I found that work, as Whitman said, "did not finally satisfy or permanently wear," yet if I was to continue to be a poet I had to labor on in order to find time to satisfy my habit.

When I first pondered a career as a poet I was easily intimidated. Robert Frost, T. S. Eliot, Ezra Pound, Elizabeth Bishop, William Carlos Williams, Wallace Stevens, Marianne Moore, Archibald MacLeish, W. H. Auden, Theodore Roethke, Robert Lowell, Muriel Rukeyser, John Berryman, Richard Wilbur, W. S. Merwin, and a host of other significant poets were alive and writing in English. Dylan Thomas, Wilfred Owen, D. H. Lawrence, and Hart Crane should have been alive. The ghost of Yeats was very much at large. It was presumptuous to even dream about mounting a career in poetry, but I was young and all things seemed possible. It never occurred to me that I might end up a publisher of poetry as well.

I was not an attentive student and failed my first year of college. I went to work in a steel mill and after a year was drafted. Under these unlikely conditions I decided to be a poet. When I was discharged I tried college again on the GI Bill. I had to scramble hard to make up for my poor record, and there were periods when I had to leave school and hold modest jobs. Once I worked for a year as a Commercial Credit adjuster. Four doors down from our office there was a bookstore where I spent my lunch hours and preserved my sanity. My parents were understandably concerned and not heartened when I spent a portion of each paycheck on poetry books.

When I was not haunting bars, I lurked in my attic room reading slender clothbound editions. I worked hard, harassing many a poor debtor in order to earn my money so I could buy these precious objects. I loved to stroke their tight, handsome bindings, open them to the redolence of paper and ink. I have read poetry all my adult life, but this was my most magical period. It was all pristine and delicious. Uninhibited by criticism, I swallowed the books whole, dazzled even by the obscurities.

I still have these venerable volumes, cherish them, take them down from my shelves from time to time and stroke them. I open the pages and look at my youthful markings, reaching back to that time when I was so puerile and uncertain, intending to be a poet without having any idea what this really meant.

The books were published by refined, distant New York and Boston trade houses. I was fascinated even by their magical logos: the Random House house, Henry Holt's owl, Farrar's fish, Liveright's scriber, Houghton-Mifflin's boy on a dolphin, Harper's torch, Little, Brown's Poseidon, Knopf's borzoi, Scribner's lamp. Elegantly designed, flawlessly printed, and bound with rich, sweet-smelling cloth—I cherished them more than my catcher's mitt, even my jazz records.

I recall reading an article in the erstwhile *Saturday Review of Literature* about how these venerable firms did not publish poetry for profit, but out of a sense of cultural obligation. Sales of their best-selling fiction and nonfiction covered some costs of this more speculative literary publishing. It astonished me that in this resourceful, teeming world, these great poets could not earn their own way. It seemed to me that their books should sell better than Chevrolets. But only Frost and Sandburg showed modest profits; the rest did well to break even. I was greatly impressed that these cultured houses believed that tasteful, artistic publishing was a social responsibility.

When young Theodore Roethke's poems started receiving attention in literary magazines in the late 1930s, he got a letter from an editor at Macmillan inquiring if he had a full manuscript of poems ready for consideration. Roethke sadly had to say no, but did so with some confidence that commercial publishers would be ready to read his work when the time came. This story now seems more an obscure legend than literary history.

In the late 1950s Suzanne and I married and moved to California to begin our adult lives. A series of frabjous jobs led me to a position as order filler in a wholesale book warehouse. I was very happy to be touching thousands of books every day. I paid attention, worked hard, made certain that my bosses noticed me. In a short while I was promoted to manager, and in a few years this led to a job running the book departments for Macy's Bay Area stores.

For a brief period I became corporate, posing as a young man in three-piece suit and straw hat, with a newspaper tucked under my arm, as if I had just come in from the racetrack. But I still worked hard on my poems in the evenings.

Sometimes I'd slip down to North Beach and haunt the beatnik bars after work, observing the freewheeling writers and
literary life. It seemed so liberated, so artistic, so beatific, as
they used to say. I was not living a poet's life—but I could
never figure out how to join the party. I did not know how to
schmooze, nor did I have time to hang around.

There was a great deal of posturing and most of the writing
was very bad, but I kept hearing of a young poet named Gary
Snyder. Everyone spoke of him with awe and respect. I attended
his readings and bought his books at City Lights. His range
and achievement were imposing. When Suzanne and I roamed
the evenings in North Beach, haunting the jazz and folk clubs,
occasionally we would see him with his friends, and it was no
small envy I felt.

Early one summer evening after work I felt compelled to
escape the plastic tombs and droning escalators of Macy's,
caught the cable car up over Nob Hill, and walked down into
North Beach in my dark blue three-piece suit and tie. I went to
a beatnik hangout called The Place for a draft beer, to let the
corporate life work its toxic way out of my pores. At the bar I
suddenly realized that Gary Snyder was sitting on the next
stool. He was talking to some women, but it occurred to me
that, if I was patient, I might have an opportunity to introduce
myself. Maybe we could even talk about poetry. At least I could
tell him that I admired him.

I needed a drink to screw up my courage and finally got the
bartender's attention. He had been working hard at ignoring
me. When I asked for a draft beer, he coldly looked me up and
down—my three-piecer, straw hat tilted back on my head, my
clean-shaven, rosy cheeks. Conversations in the immediate
area stalled in anticipation. Several more times the bartender
ran his frozen eyes over me, then loudly, disdainfully, he said,
"We don't have any clean glasses." There was nothing to do. My
head hung, my straw hat in my hand, I withdrew.

Out of my experience at Macy's I was appointed manager of the massive UCLA bookstore. I was twenty-nine years old and had fifty people working for me. It was a large, complex operation and I was much resented—more a referee than manager. We bought a house in the San Fernando Valley and every day I crawled onto the freeway in our Volkswagen bus, driving forty-five minutes each way, planning my escape as I gazed at the shattered safety glass on the shoulders and waited for traffic jams to loosen. I knew I did not want to spend the rest of my life retailing books in Los Angeles. I wanted to publish them, but the prospect of tackling commercial publishing in New York or Boston with no experience and a small family was daunting.

At UCLA I became attracted to the variety and erudition of university press lists. In the late 1960s and 1970s the scholarly press world was expanding rapidly and it was possible to get a job without actual book-publishing experience. My work as a book retailer was enough to land me a job as marketing manager for the University of Pittsburgh Press.

We loaded up possessions, our two kids, all the poetry books, and nursed our old VW bus across the country in 1967 to the Golden Triangle. Imagine my delight when Fred Hetzel, the director of the press, informed me that he had recently arranged to publish annual prize-winning books of poetry sponsored by the International Poetry Forum. In addition to my duties selling and promoting the press's scholarly books, I was to be administrative editor for a series of first poetry books, and was to help the poet Samuel Hazo, director of the forum, screen the manuscripts. James Dickey, William Meredith, and Abbie Huston Evans were to select the winner of the thousand-dollar United States Award from a group of finalists. I was seeing stars.

We carried a small table into my office on the thirty-third floor of the Cathedral of Learning, and the beleaguered university postal workers began trucking manuscripts up the freight elevator twice a day. Soon they had to deliver four times a day. The little table was swamped, and piles began to mount on the floor. Hundreds arrived daily—full manuscripts of poetry, at least fifty pages each—the stacks pouring out eventually into the hallway outside my office.

I called Samuel Hazo and warned him that our task was mounting. By the end of the submission period we had received a thousand submissions. Late one afternoon he slipped gingerly into the caverns of manuscripts. I had been daily witness to this gradual inundation, but he was forced to swallow it in a single gulp. I doubt that anyone had ever beheld so much unpublished poetry at one time. It was an awesome sight. He sat down on a stack of manuscripts and rubbed his forehead.

"Sam," I suggested quietly, "we'd better start reading."

Somehow we shoveled all that coal with reasonable efficiency, and Dickey, Meredith, and Evans picked James Den Boer's *Learning the Way* as the 1967 winner of the United States Award of the International Poetry Forum. We published his book and two runners-up, which we selected from the finalists—Jon Anderson's *Looking for Jonathan* and John Engels's *The Homer Mitchell Place.*

How proud I was of these books, caressing them like beautiful children in their lovely clothbound and paperbound editions. As they arrived from the printer, I opened them and let their sweetness drift up to my nostrils. I admired them all and was enormously proud of my part in what we had done.

In following years we published the winning first collections of David Young, Shirley Kaufman, Richard Shelton, and Larry Levis, and a host of splendid runners-up—but after five years of coping with the awkward system of committee judging, we decided to go with a single final judge. Muriel Rukeyser agreed to serve. She asked how many manuscripts we expected. I could not imagine, having rejected thousands of manuscripts over past years, that we would have that kind of volume again, so I told her that probably five hundred would come in.

By the end of the submission period we had reached new heights. There were thirteen hundred manuscripts and, yes, they were all stacked in and outside my office. As I sat at my desk I could hear the muses groaning under the sheer weight of submission. My colleagues had to stand when they visited my office.

I called Muriel Rukeyser in New York and told her what had happened. When she recovered and could hear again, I strongly suggested that I begin screening manuscripts in Pittsburgh and hire some other poets to help. No, she said, recovering her estimable strength and resolve. She wanted to do the whole job, to screen them all herself.

"But, Miss Rukeyser," I said, "thirteen hundred!"

"You may call me Muriel. *All* of them," she said firmly. But Muriel was in New York and the manuscripts were in Pittsburgh.

After much discussion with Fred Hetzel, we decided on an experiment. We would fly Muriel to Pittsburgh for a weekend to read manuscripts. I lugged a hundred manuscripts up to her hotel room and gave her my home phone number to call when she was ready for more. But no call came, and late Sunday when I arrived at the hotel, I found that she had gone through thirty-four manuscripts.

Clearly this was not the answer. I appealed to her again as I drove her to the airport. "*All* of them!" she said.

Hetzel felt it would be irresponsible to chance shipping all the manuscripts to New York, so I did the only thing possible. I rented a U-Haul truck, personally lugged all the manuscripts onto the freight elevator, descended the thirty-three floors to the loading dock, and toted them out to the truck. I bravely waved good-bye to my family and set out across Pennsylvania for Manhattan with, I'll wager, the greatest concentrated load of poesy ever hauled across the United States. The springs of the truck were squawking in iambic pentameter.

I pulled into a truck stop for coffee and the driver parked in a rig next to mine came over and asked me what I was hauling. I looked him over carefully. His arms weren't tattooed, but he was a considerable figure. I deliberated for a few moments. I was young then, cocky and indestructible.

"Poetry," I said.

I'll hand it to him. He didn't blink, but his response was not immediate. Finally, in mock earnestness, he said, "Is that a fact! Well say, fellow, I've got a load of ballet slippers in here."

I skipped the coffee and moved on. When I reached New York it was all I could do to resist an impulse to drive to the shore and somehow plunge the whole poetic load into the Atlantic, becoming an American culture hero. But dutifully I breasted upper Manhattan traffic, hauling my cargo to the offices of the American Academy and Institute of Arts and Letters, where Muriel had arranged to use an empty office. I borrowed a hand truck from the storage room and began unloading.

As I sweated at my task, another burly guy came up and announced, "Sorry, bud. That's our work." He was from the Teamsters union, the buildings in the area were organized, and he was not going to let me unload my poetry. He and his helpers were to do the job and be paid union wages. The academy was not about to assume this charge, so I shelled out my last cash to the Teamsters and wired home for more.

The men were friendly as they worked. One of them asked, "What are we handling here?" Now I must admit that sometimes I am not the swiftest person, but I retain enough judgment not to tempt the fates twice in one day. "Demolition diagrams," I told him. "They are demolition diagrams."

I received many calls from Muriel over the next few months, sometimes in the middle of the night. She wanted to discuss certain manuscripts, give me progress reports; she asked for more money and anguished over the work. I found more money but suggested that we hire someone in New York to help her screen. No. She would read *all* of them. When she didn't call, I worried, and called her. The strain was evident despite her amazing strength and determination. She wanted to *do* this. It was for poetry, and nothing was more important. As she went along she wrote a note about each manuscript— sometimes just one word, but a very evocative word: *bathroom, heaven, bed-bouncing, Dr. Doolittle, English Department.* In the midst of all this, she continued her strenuous political activism. At one point she was arrested at a demonstration and had to suffer the indignities of going to jail. She kept calling me, and her talk and concerns became more disturbing.

At last she phoned and grandly announced, "We have our winner. It is an extraordinary effort by a young poet named Marc Weber."

The manuscript was called *48 Small Poems,* and, indeed, they were forty-eight very small poems. I read them all several times, and they grew smaller—young ramblings about family, growing up, protesting, feeling the cold, girls, making love, drinking and tripping, camping out, being an English major. Marc Weber was twenty-one years old, living in Colorado. He had some talent, but these were early, immature ruminations, acceptable classroom work—no punctuation, no capitalization, no titles, the language conversational and bunched up to look "mysterious."

What on earth? I called Muriel and asked to see the runners-up, disguising my request by telling her we were looking for other finalists to publish. When I read the other manuscripts she had selected they were all fine, accomplished work, far superior to the winner. So her marvelous eye hadn't completely failed her. I picked two especially good ones and, after much nervous rumination, called her. I was in no position to do this:

Muriel had worked so long and driven herself to exhaustion. I held onto my hat and asked her to reread these manuscripts along with Weber's, and to give her decision a little more time. She was amazingly considerate in her abruptness but in no uncertain terms slammed me back into my place.

We published *48 Small Poems* as the 1972 winner of the United States Award. It wasn't Marc Weber's fault, it wasn't mine, and I don't believe it was Muriel's. I believe it was a sign of those curious, illusory times when, in our guilt, we indulged extreme youth and allowed ourselves to believe that baby boomers were our wise spokesmen.

To myself I said, So this is poetry editing? Did ever T. S. Eliot or John Ciardi or Stanley Burnshaw or Harriet Monroe or James Laughlin or John Hall Wheelock have to contend with such things? Is this the way Matthew Arnold or Leonard Woolf operated?

But it got better. I gained experience as an editor of poetry and learned how to control the editing process, involving myself more directly in making final decisions. I moved on from Pittsburgh to be director of the university presses at Georgia and Iowa. In each place I waited several years before starting poetry series, so I could concentrate on building a full list of scholarly and regional books.

But being able to publish over a hundred poetry books during my working career as a scholarly publisher was glorious license. My poet friends used to envy me and think I spent all my days and years reading and pondering poetry manuscripts, but I did most of my poetry editorial work in spare time on weekends and in the evenings. My real work was acquiring and overseeing the evaluation of other kinds of books. During my thirty years at three university presses I was involved in the publication of more than a thousand scholarly and regional books.

I witnessed massive changes in the book business over four decades. When I started out as a retail manager and book buyer in California, the publishers' sales representatives were frequently liberal arts graduates of schools like Brown, Dartmouth, Reed, Vanderbilt, Stanford, Oberlin, even Oxford and Cambridge. They were cultivated persons who read the books they represented and were proud of their authors. They led thoughtful and in some cases artful lives. They showed new titles with enthusiasm and intelligence. The editors I met were intellectuals, highly skilled individuals, enthusiastic about fine writing and things of the mind. With the exception of the large companies—Doubleday, McGraw-Hill, Simon & Schuster— book publishing houses were small, vibrant, eccentric, and fiercely independent businesses.

But in the mid-1960s inflation took a serious toll and these publishers began to acquiesce, selling out to larger corporations. The corporate swallowing went on apace and the older sales representatives were squeezed out or retired early, replaced by a new order—business school graduates who carried computer quota sheets and selling aids in their attaché cases. They referred to their books as "pieces," and the only thing they seemed to read were memos from enterprising, voracious sales managers. The editors and executives who occasionally came through now were like calibrated accountants. The fabled Richard Snyder visited my office when I was buying books for Macy's, and he seemed more like an ax murderer than a publisher. They all lived with the fear that sooner or later they would pick up the *Wall Street Journal* and learn that their home office had been swallowed by a larger corporate entity. The huge monopolies had no publishing sensitivity and at first regarded their new book houses as fascinating but ephemeral toys. When they did not show quick and substantial profit, the corporations shook them like delicate music boxes, and out fell the fine editors, talented designers, and sensitive management.

So in 1967, at the first signs of these developments, not only was I glad to escape the suburbs of Los Angeles, but I was pleased to move away from this feeding frenzy and establish myself in scholarly publishing—a kind of book publishing that still concerned itself more with quality than with quantity. The work was challenging, rarefied, generally underpaid, sometimes tedious and difficult, but worthy.

There are signs that this is changing. The universities that maintain the presses are becoming more corporate-like, and they begin to demand smaller deficits—even recompense—from their presses. Technology is changing scholarship and the publishing process.

Some technological pundits adamantly claim that the publication of all printed books will pass in the coming decades, giving way to electronic devices. They already sardonically refer to libraries as museums. It seems we might relinquish that once indispensable human icon of a person sitting in a quiet room reading a bound book. Johann Gutenberg developed the first printing press around 1437. Perhaps in my publishing years I was witnessing, without realizing it, the end of more than five hundred years of bookish history. If so, it was a lovely half-millennium and I am a ready mourner at the funeral.

Suzanne and I live now on our ridge top far from the madding crowd. I am concerned with family, words, grasses, trees, weather, music, birds, pictures, the state of our health, our advancing years, and, yes—as always with books. We still buy them and read them, and we will keep all of them in our own little "museum" until we die.

Library

THE BIG TWO-CAR GARAGE near our house on the ridge
became a storage space and catchall. If we pulled the truck in
during the winter, mice came out of the walls and crawled into
its warm heater vents to build nests. A blast of twigs and fuzz
hit the inside of the grates when we turned on the fan, and the
smell of mouse permeated the cab. It cost a hundred bucks to
have the vents cleaned out, so we parked outside in all weather
and used the garage for our firewood stack, a place to throw
outdoor furniture, boxes of empty jars, coils of old rope, broken lamps, ignored exercise equipment, injured bicycles. It
swarmed with mice that pitter-patted, leaving their beady
turds everywhere. I baited traps with little success, until one
day I noticed that the garage had grown quiet. Rummaging
around, I found the discarded skin of a five-foot bull snake,
which had feasted mightily for a while and outgrown itself.

Increasingly we thought about the time when we would live
on the farm permanently. The house was efficient and small,
but there was no indoor space to get away from each other,
certainly no space to put our large collection of books. One
keen autumn day we came in from a long ramble, walking
down the gravel road toward the garage when the idea struck
both of us simultaneously. We would make the garage our

library. It was an inspiration so perfect we got out the bottle of single malt scotch and toasted our ingenuity.

It took several years to gather the money and ingratiate ourselves with a good local contractor. There are contractors and carpenters, and then there are odd jobbers in the countryside. We decided we wanted none of the latter for our library. We asked neighbors for advice and got bids from contractors who were willing to look at the job. We selected Barney Gunderson.

The structure already existed and we had no plans or blueprints, so we described our vision for the renovation to the bidders. Only Barney appeared to listen carefully, and his price was reasonable. When we called him with our happy decision he said, "'kay, guess I can do it about right."

We set a date—but after a five-month hiatus we began to be concerned. "We're going to get right on that," he'd say when I called.

It is impossible to duplicate Barney's talk with its gestures and grimaces. The fact that we didn't understand him added to our uneasiness. He would say something like, "We got to sink them four-by-fours for the carport deep to hold them struts to keep them four-by-eight-by-three-quarter slabs up and them animals out. That way on it. When we got that bugger in we like to stud it into the garage whackers solid so's there's no wobble. That way on it. And if we set them big glass doors in you want, we got to reinforce with studs doubled-up and beared so there's no wind sucking on them babies."

"What?" we would say, looking nervously at each other.

"Don't worry. We got it."

"Okay, okay."

"It goes in nice that way," Barney would say. "That way on it."

When he finally appeared half a year after the agreed-upon starting time, we were worn-out with uneasiness. We heard him jabbering to his helpers and had no idea what was being communicated. When they started yanking off old siding and pitching it violently into piles, we felt like fishermen caught in a storm. We didn't want to stand around wringing our hands, so finally we waved good-bye and drove back to Iowa City. It was not a courageous thing to do—and it didn't seem prudent.

Two weeks later Barney called and said, "Job's done. We had to do some baffle-bustin' on that carport connection, but she looks pretty good." We drove up in silence, both of us squirming in quiet trepidation.

It was beautiful—far handsomer than we had imagined. In fact, Barney was the one with imagination. His innovations were splendid and tasteful. We thanked him with enthusiasm and wrote the final check.

"She's not too bad," he admitted. "Them old corners was punked-up, so we changed 'em as we go. Sumbitch who did that early work didn't seal good. No extra charge. That way on it."

"Okay, okay," we said, happy as old Folger when the last brick went into the Shakespeare library.

Now the library is one of our great joys, shelved floor to ceiling on all walls with thousands of books and crammed with our beloved stuff: collections, artifacts, keepsakes; big flat drawers full of prints and photographs; busts of Mozart, Dumas, Shakespeare, Dante, Wagner, Blake; bottles of sherry and brandy; magnificent music on CDs and tapes; good lamps and comfortable chairs. We look up from our books and gaze out the big windowed entrance all the way up the gravel road and fields to the old pump on the horizon. Sunsets beam down across the ridge right through our door.

The library might sound opulent, but these are treasures only to us, lovingly accumulated for half a century. Richie Halverson stepped into the library only once. He already knew he had eccentric neighbors. I think he found it claustrophobic. He was as mystified by it as I am by his milking shed. Certainly he did not want to spend a lot of time thinking about why, in the name of heaven, we would want such a thing. The eye of the beholder.

"I promised Nora I would go in with her for groceries," he said and quickstepped back out the door.

I continue to struggle with my work ethic. In my retirement, I still feel guilty if I read a book in the middle of the day. I can look at manuscripts because that is "work," but books are for pleasure. At the state universities where I worked, if administrators were seen reading books during working hours, it was felt that they were loafing. Okay for faculty—sometimes—but the staff was supposed to stay busy.

Now, on the farm, in warm weather I still tend to stay occupied with outdoor chores after my writing hours, and I read in the evenings. But increasingly I go to the library during the days, especially in winter and on very hot summer days. I always announce to Suzanne, "I'm going to the library," somehow feeling the need to confess my indolence to someone.

I suspect that when I can no longer easily walk the half mile up the road to my writing shack, I will take up scribbling in a corner of the library. I've already tried it on some very bad weather days, but it requires discipline. My shack is mostly barren: a few pictures, reference books, table, my Jackie Robinson bat, electric heater and fan, typewriter and small computer, the chest of drawers and rug where our dog Sheba perches to look out the window. But when I work in the library it is full of distractions—things that interest me. Each time I move my eyes, I see something I want to look at or an object or book that evokes memories.

The library is a culmination of many things for both of us. In the houses we owned over the years, our books and papers were scattered, stashed in nooks and crannies, in attics and basements, bedrooms and small studies. It is a joy and a comfort to bring them together. Now we nest happily like two old birds in the midst of the gatherings of our lifetimes. It is a place for peace.

Insects and Arachnids

It is difficult to remain at peace with certain kinds of insects. I enforce a rule I made for myself: I share the outdoors with them but, just as they do not tolerate my encroachment on their nests and space, I will not permit their invasion of my dwellings. It seems a reasonable arrangement.

I make no deals, however, with insects whose existence depends on sucking my blood. Mosquitoes are voracious and legion in humid weather. We use mild lotions and sprays to keep them somewhat at bay. We are constantly swatting. I cannot imagine what life was like in warm weather before these preventatives were developed. Mosquitoes attacked Lewis and Clark's party in thick, relentless clouds, gnawing at their ears, noses, eyes, throats, and hands. The men stood in the smoke of their campfires at night and coated their exposed flesh with voyager's grease to keep them away. When they were rowing or portaging and their hands were occupied, they had no choice but to let their flesh be ravaged. Even now, with all our sprays, mists, fumes, and potions, mosquitoes can rout our picnics or cause hasty retreats from damp areas of the woods. We cover flesh as much as we can stand in the heat and dose heavily for our berry-picking expeditions.

Ticks are another problem, and we make no concessions.

But they are quieter, more insidious little beasts. We treat our bushy-haired dog, Sheba, with a preventative, but despite our vigilance we are constantly picking engorged tick carcasses out of her thick fur. We put strong deterrents on our ankles and wrists and check each other regularly to detect their sneaky little attachments.

Being a new country person, I found stinging insects threatening. When I lived in towns I avoided hornets, wasps, and bees. The only times they came to my mind were the rare occasions when I received their painful stings. Now they are part of my life and I worry when I don't see them. It is more than tolerance; it is a kind of cohosting. I let them build nests under the eaves of the house and my writing shack, as long as they are out of the way, and I only interfere with their existence when occasionally they find their way inside our dwellings.

But at first we had an uneasy peace. There were huge, very active wasp and hornet nests on the cornices of the house when we moved in, and one especially large one in the eaves of what was then the garage. Our children and grandchildren were coming to visit and I wanted no painful accidents. I bought a can of streak spray insecticide and, like a fool, in broad daylight stood back and hit the nest with a shot. It rang like a gong and exploded—suddenly the air was stippled with furious hornets zipping in every direction. I backstepped quickly and ducked around the garage. Amazingly, I received no stings.

Humbled by the damage I had caused, and the ferocity and power of the hornets' eruption from the nest, I put away the can of poison and rethought my position. I've used the spray only a few times since for minor patrols—when they started building nests in doorways, for instance—and I use it at dusk when they are dormant. I let them be, and have only been stung a dozen times since we've lived here. It always makes me furious, but then I calm down. The incidents are isolated.

Hornets and wasps are more truculent at the end of summer when they know their work is done and their time is nigh, but I give them ground and keep my eyes on them. It is a reasonable truce.

In sunny weather our flowered meadows are alive with the motions and flights of bees, grasshoppers, crickets, and butterflies. They sweep aside in great waves when we trudge through the high hay. Grasshoppers come in hordes during dry periods and damage the clover and hay. Richie Halverson says they seem to pinch the clover and oats, sucking on them and turning them yellow before their time.

In mid to late summer butterflies are legion, the air full of their delirious chasing and courting—monarchs, viceroys, orange and yellow sulfurs, and many species we don't identify. There are pairs with colored spots that reverse on the wings, the opposites seeming to attract each other. There are exquisite black ones with jagged wings like bats.

During one morning walk a frisky monarch followed us and batted around our heads, dipping in and out as if to play. Sheba kept leaping at it, and it seemed to enjoy the game of dodge. I put out my finger to see if I could get it to perch, but it whisked away frolicking, then came back to whirl around again as if it wanted to tease us.

In September the yellow sulfurs dance in the brisk air and make sweet signs to each other. We find parties of them along the gravel road, formed in circles, fluttering and flirting. When we come too close, they all fly up, matching in twos and threes, chasing each other, then descend to circle and revel some more. It is like *A Midsummer Night's Dream*. We love to watch them lift in multitudes over the fields and roads, flittering high, then descending to spangle the hay. Months later when we trudge out into the cold winter fields, we imagine we see their rapturous spirits risen through layers of drifts to sparkle on the snow crust.

Later in autumn we see monarchs on warm days, quivering and dying, but still with enough juice left to fly up if we approach. We found a large monarch gasping its last in the gravel, flapping around as its life drained away. We were able to look at it closely, picked it up and held it so we could see the sun through its wings, perceiving how ancient artisans first got the idea for the glories of stained glass.

As with wasps and hornets, I have made a settlement with spiders as well, although I still give them plenty of ground. It is more respect than distaste. They love my writing shack. I grant them the whole outdoors, even the inside corners of my windows, a few nooks here and there, and the tops of books. This seems fair enough to me. I appreciate that they snare flies and mosquitoes, but I don't want them sneaking around under my desk, and I *will* dispatch them if I find their webs in my work area. I've been bitten in the past and it makes me feel bad.

There was a prolific hatching of spiders in my writing shack once, and hundreds of the new ones spread out on the ceiling to air out their tiny bodies. There are still marks of my great battle with them, as one by one I daubed them out with a tissue. Even at this very early stage they were amazingly deft, dropping down on minute strands to avoid disaster when I reached for them. I considered feeling guilty about this but concluded that I did not want my precious writing space creeping with spiders.

We see some amazing spider specimens outdoors; the most spectacular are yellow and black striped ones that web on milkweed pods or mullein. There are gray fuzzy ones as big as cockleburs that, I am sure, would not hesitate for a moment to put their fangs in me if I blundered into them. I saw one of the former struggling in a surprise April snow, trying somehow to stay warm enough to live. I considered dropping my handkerchief over it, but our truce does not include my giving them deliverance.

Grasses, Fruits, Plants

T READ, CUT, RIP, cement, burn, insult the grass; it returns
and abides. You destroy grass only by asking too much of it,
then it leaves you with a sorry face of dust. Slash of blades,
teeth of animals, fire and water. It comes back. Fescue, rye,
bamboo, clover, corn, reed, broom, bluestem, rice, cane, timothy, barley, wheat, foxtail, milo, flax, grain—just a small part of
the list. Grass can grow over your head and make you disappear, can cover your house if you neglect it, swarm over your
bed. It is your food and your poison. Like the sky, it covers you
when you die. Try to ignore it, but always it is under your feet,
comes back through cracks in cement, out of ashes and dead
earth, swarming over its own dead. It is triumphant in rain
and sunlight, patient under snow and ice. Root, tuber, vein,
blade, spike, node, sheath, floret, bundle, hollow stems, and
joints where its leaves are attached. Over 235 genera, nine thousand species. Grass is long lists. It is more than the stars you
can see in the sky.

   The green on our ridge is unabashed in warm weather, but
except for trees, there is very little of the area's original vegetation. The nonnative grasses in the thirty acres of hay fields are
managed and rotated. Richie Halverson and his family have
been farming them in a similar way for close to a hundred

years. He goes from hay—alfalfa, timothy, and clover—to corn, then to oats, then back to hay. But with or without his management, the grasses are indomitable.

As managed by Richie, the cropped fields become almost geometric in their ripe loveliness. I mow slender paths on the edges so we can walk near the woods. When the grass is high and a breeze is up, it is like walking on rolling, undulating water. A parting spray of insects and toads rolls off to each side as we amble. The green grasses and clover are so rich and delicious looking; if I were a cow I would want to eat them like ice cream. The ripening timothy is a warm, lilting color—rust brown, yellow, and at least two shades of green, a vision in the sun. The mature oats hover between yellow and tan and glow like precious metal in the light.

When we walk between rows of corn in late summer, we are sealed into a different dimension; things are orderly and green within those dim, verdant walls, urgently growing moment by moment. I believe that if I tuned my hearing aids properly, I could hear driven cells in the fibers groaning and urgently splitting.

In spring, sunlight is held in an outburst of dandelions. Queen Anne's lace invades the fields, brushing and sopping our jeans as we walk. Patches of thistle appear, their light-purple blossoms almost beckoning, yet if I look closely I see they are barbed and ominous. They are so tenacious and pervasive; they must be controlled, yet one pays a harsh physical price for removing them.

Solitary mullein plants dominate their surroundings; the big woolly leaves host spider webs, and clustered yellow flowers become small brown cups when their blossoming ends. We learned that old people used to dip the dried plants in tallow and use them as torches, but we have never tried this.

My favorite "weed" is chicory, its sky blue so pleasing to my eye. It holds along the roadside and soothes us in our walks.

Late in summer it fades like old clothes, becoming almost pink. The blossoms tighten at night, taking themselves in like washing, then appear again cobalt blue in first light and hang out to dry. I love the shape of the flower and the singular way the stems grow in angles and pieces. If I could paint, I would always include the blue of chicory in my pictures. If I could play tenor saxophone, I would play those delicate blues. If I could dance, I would unfold and be as light as those blossoms.

We have a shifting crop of blackberries, gooseberries, and red and black raspberries along our fields and dirt roads. Conditions are paramount. We can never predict where the fullest crops will grow, or which bushes will flourish. When the time comes for picking we gird ourselves with long-sleeved shirts and thick pants in the heat, sweating and wading into the bushes like bears. Despite our precautions we still come out bloodied. But the berries are worth our suffering. They draw us into their brambles with their irresistible ripeness. Their colors against the green foliage are luminescent and vivid, made to attract birds and animals; but they excite us, too, drawing us deeper into the patches, attracted by sightings of still plumper berries, scourging ourselves as we reach like Tantalus for them. Mosquitoes feast on our ears and cheeks. In our excitement we pay little attention to where we step, trusting that we won't put a foot down into a gopher hole or on a bee's nest or a snake. Gleefully we tote our pickings home and fill the house with the heavenly odor of berries simmering as we prepare our jams.

When we walk in a far area of our quiet fields or woods, I imagine what it is like when we are not present. The silence is medieval and long, extending for weeks or months. When we appear, chattering and barging along with our dog, we are defilement. When we depart, the silence returns, interrupted only by the rustling of birds and animals, the whine of insects, and light breezes in the treetops.

We will miss the orderliness of the crops in the fields, the squares and rectangles of managed pastel colors, but we are going to put our fields into a set-aside program next year. Then we will see much more of the local wildflowers and flowering weeds—purple ironweed, bergamot, daisies, primroses, violets, yellow pie flowers, buttercups, fleabane, forget-me-nots, asters, and others we will train ourselves to identify. But then, perhaps it is not so important that we learn their names. We toy with the idea of planting some portion of the fields in native grasses and wildflowers, but the task is daunting and risks our pact with silence. The land has been managed for decades by farmers. The idea of the set-aside program is to let it rest. What is done, is done.

Gardening

*And they heard the voice of the Lord God walking in the garden in
the cool of the day: and Adam and his wife hid themselves from
the presence of the Lord God amongst the trees of the garden.*

Genesis 3:8

SUZANNE AND I came to our ridge top with full knowledge
of good and evil. We weren't hiding from the Lord God. We
did not know at the time, but we had been waiting all our lives
to be in this garden place, and no serpent was going to trick us
out of it at this late date.

At first it was only weekends, but then retirement was
thrust upon us. The scene is entirely ours, we hear no sounds
but our own and those of creatures in our woods and meadows. In winter we look out a long way through bare woods to
distant silos and church steeples. In warm months we are
enclosed in the foliage of trees. We toil in our garden, paying
for Adam and Eve's violation. They did not have to drudge in
Eden; it was presented full grown to them. Now every time our
backs ache, we are paying for their transgression. We call our
spade and hoe Adam and Eve.

Aging gardeners must nurture a vision. Our arches, backs,
shoulders, and knees ache. Shovel and lift, break clods, rake

smooth, lift stones, cut borders, plant seed, bend and bend—
everything black and brown. We must hold a dream in our
boiling heads. The supreme garden visionary, Monet, rarely
put his hand on a spade when he got older. He banished black
and brown from his pallet as if they reminded him of travail.
Cézanne described him as "only an eye, but my God what an
eye!"

I shovel and heave, chop and chop like a good peasant. I
have a few modest visions as my back aches, but I have never,
never become an eye. And I never cease resenting the carelessness of the first man and woman. Yet gardens have always been
part of my life.

Wham, bam went the siding, beating like a drum, resounding
through the old garage. I was a hot, surly teenager, throwing
shovelfuls of dirt against the corrugated steel, making it rumble, to be certain my family was aware of my misery. I lifted
large stones from the wheelbarrow and dropped them into the
dirt, then slammed in more dirt.

My mother had a vision—and she had a son. She wanted a
rock garden placed against the old garage to make it look better, and had at last coerced my help. Like that of most very
young people, my mode was existential; I breathed only for the
moment—no history, no future, no vision of color and beauty
in my mind. I only wanted to take immediate pleasure with
friends on this glorious Sunday afternoon in Ohio. I did not
know moss rose, phlox, rock cress, nor did I care a smidgen of
dirt about pinks.

Months later, in late summer, I was dashing from the house
out the back way past the garage when something caught the
corner of my eye and stopped me. The rock garden had
bloomed and I was astounded by color. I looked and looked,
and it was beautiful. I was surprised by my sense of pride
and accomplishment. Recalling my petulance, I was ashamed,

but I never admitted this to my mother or the Lord God.
I hurried on.

My parents favored an old, now forgotten custom: the Sunday
drive. I tried to escape these outings, but there were no
excuses; my father commanded our presence. Frequently we
took day trips to area gardens, strolling, sniffing, and gazing at
blossoms. There were luxurious lilac gardens in Kent, which
we toured annually in the spring, savoring the wash of pastel
purples, pinks, and whites, and glorying in the sublime aroma.
An older woman owned the big house and gardens and did
most of the work. She always seemed weary, sitting out on the
benches chatting with her Sunday visitors. Once I sat down
with her and she described the rigors of pruning and fertiliz-
ing, saying she wished I lived in Kent so I could help her. I was
polite about this but did not share her wish. I saw no sense in
what she did. The percentages were not good—toiling eleven
months to exist for a month in fairyland.

When my parents grew elderly they gave up their Sunday
garden drives, closed their old flowerbeds, and seeded them
with grass. They did only small gardening, potting a few plants
and tending small patches. Their pleasure became walking to
the newly established garden center in the park near our
house. After mass they strolled through the neighborhood,
across the railroad track, down verdant park paths to a bridge
crossing the creek, on to the wide beds and greenhouse of the
center. They reported their pleasure and excitement in letters
they sent to me in California. My father especially seemed to
enjoy looking at other people's flowers.

I have carried this garden heritage to all my homes and
travels—to San Francisco, Los Angeles, Pittsburgh, Georgia,
Iowa, China, France, Germany, Great Britain, Canada, and now
to Soldiers Grove in the driftless hills of southwestern Wisconsin. Wherever I wandered I toured the gardens. Once,

walking in London's venerable Kew Gardens late on a Sunday
afternoon, I turned a corner and came across a middle-aged
couple kissing passionately on a bench under a flowering
hawthorn. It was a great tradition. Medieval French engravers
often portrayed "love gardens" with lovers dallying everywhere
in the posies. It was a sweet scene and I was happy for the couple, hurrying to pass and leave them to their loving. But when
they sensed my presence they pushed apart guiltily. The
woman looked away, but I could see that she was beautiful.
The man, very substantial in a three-piece suit, looked at me in
shock. I must have resembled someone he knew, and he was
worried I might recognize him.

All pleasure suddenly passed, the beauty of the tree, the
passion of their kiss, and my gladness for them. Obviously
they were guilty under the blossoms, and I regretted that I had
turned the corner to remind them. A garden is a good place to
kiss—but apparently not this kiss. "And they heard the voice of
the Lord God walking in the garden in the cool of the day..."

Gardens not only welcome lovers; they encourage the expression of beauty. The tradition has been constant from the
earliest flower daubs of cave people through impressionist
glories to photography.

Just after the turn of the last century, the means for making
color photographs was invented. Photographers began setting
up tripods in gardens. These first color images, called auto-
chromes, are positives on glass. The basic material was
mundane—from the garden, in fact: potatoes dried and pul-
verized, the particles separated and dyed in three primary
colors, red-orange, green, and blue-violet, spread on the plates
with a sticky varnish. When they were processed, the pictures
were soft, luminous, like miniature neoimpressionist paintings, as if light existed on bright dust motes hovering in color,
a glimmer of how the garden of Eden must have looked to

Adam and Eve. Flowers bloom in these images, drudgery is done, there is only the pleasure of beholding color and shape. Black and brown are banished. This is the kind of vision a gardener must hold in his mind when his back is aching.

When the dream ends, the garden goes back to being unrelieved toil and pain. It is our punishment. Hieronymus Bosch, half a millennium ago, created his recondite triptych of the Garden of Earthly Delights. The passage goes from the glories and delights of Eden on the left panel, to the strange, often cruel, erotic activities, hideous plants, and evil fruits of the fecund garden in the middle, to the devastated garden and combative, furious fires of hell on earth on the right. In a milder sense, our gardens represent this passage from germinal innocence to boundless pullulation to corruption, devastation, and death.

Mrs. Scheffley was very old and disturbed, growling and shrieking at us boys whenever we came near her dreary house with its ruined garden of riotous, untended vegetation. She was skeletal and wore dark, tattered long dresses, but one could see in her face that she had once been fair—which made her anger even more daunting.

"Stay away from there," my mother said. She told me that the huge yard had once been a magnificent garden, Mrs. Scheffley's pride. But when her husband died she became inconsolable and unapproachable, letting the place go wild as she descended into desolate withdrawal. There were still traces of its former glory: overgrown ledges, skeletons of trellises being slowly pulled down by swarming vines, places where weeds washed over the stones of what had been a rock garden, odd flashes of color here and there where bulbs and perennials held their ground. But the place was now savage and untended, except for a cleared space in the middle, where Mrs. Scheffley burned trash.

Her son still lived in the house with her, but he was a miserable creature. Discharged abruptly by the army, he had a fetish for young boys. He frequently tried to give us money or candy. We heard rumors of his activities, how he lured lads up to his room and attempted to fondle them. We stayed away from him, but he tried to talk us into wrestling matches, claiming he wanted to show us the jujitsu he had learned in the army. Once Fat Carlson, who thought he was tough, took him on in the tattered garden, but Scheffley groped him until Fat broke loose and we all ran away. When Scheffley went back into the gray, peeling house, we returned to throw stones, until Mrs. Scheffley came out and wailed her misery at us.

Sometimes in warm weather, when the windows were open, we could hear her berating him loudly. Eventually some boys told on him and he was incarcerated. Mrs. Scheffley became even wilder when we came near, attempting to throw stones at us with an awkward, stiff-elbowed motion as she snapped her dentures and shrieked.

One Sunday I was riding my bicycle along the alley that ran behind her house and heard wild howling. I thought that perhaps a dog had gotten into her trash. I crawled through dense brush at the back of her yard, saw a fire burning in her trash pit, and, lying near it, what seemed to be a piece of smoking meat browned by the fire. As I crept nearer, the thing lifted its head and screamed. It was Mrs. Scheffley. Her long dress had caught fire and, amid the wreckage of her garden, every part of her had been burned except the tortured blossom of her face. In that moment Mrs. Scheffley and I looked at each other with the only understanding we ever shared. Her garden had died years before, and now the last immense cruelty had been inflicted. I knew that I was somehow part of the cruelty, but I had a last chance.

I did not know how to help her, but in my horror began loudly crying out until neighbors came to her aid. Then I ran away home and hid in my room. In a while I heard the ambulance hurrying through the neighborhood.

Her house stayed empty through the rest of my childhood and I never went near her place again. Even years later when I visited my parents and we ambled through the neighborhood down through the park to look at the blossoms in the flower center, I always made certain we avoided the street where Mrs. Scheffley's house and ruined garden had stood.

My parents did not live long enough to see our ridge-top farm in southwest Wisconsin. I regret this because it is the kind of place they yearned for all their lives. They would have been happy for us. Suzanne and I don't have the time, energy, or means to landscape and create formal beds; but this place is a garden with all its tranquility, vision, work, and blooming. Somehow through long toil and even bombast, we seem to have edged back to the first panel of Bosch's triptych.

Our days are as we wish them: quiet hours for writing and thinking in the morning, then a long walk with the dog, lunch, and a nap. In good weather we tend our modest vegetable garden and do chores in the afternoon. It is a lifelong dream come true.

I was pulling down an old woodpile, setting up some logs to split for our winter fires, and found a large ribbon garter snake that had taken up residence between some pieces of wood. Too frightened and surprised to make a fuss, he slipped out to the grass and squirmed to hide in a large pile of old elm bark.

The next day when I came out to split more wood he was coiled on top of his new residence, watching me, his head raised, tongue jabbing in and out. I think he was trying to talk to me, but his voice was thin and I have been hard of hearing for many years.

Coyotes, Foxes, Wolves

Unloading the pickup one evening I heard a sudden, tumultuous yipping followed by a chorus of long howls from near the old pump up the road. An even more spirited and shrill soprano response came from the south side woods. I stopped hauling and sat down on the tailgate. The ritual exchange was made several times. Then, as if they had been waiting their turn, all dogs within earshot started to bark.

This was my first time as an audience for coyote music. I was mildly alarmed because it sounded like a barbarian attack and I seemed to be surrounded. But I remembered Richie Halverson telling me that it only takes two or three coyotes to raise a considerable commotion.

One evening we were taking our after-dinner constitutional on the road, walking on the upgrade just past my writing shack, when the quiet was violated by an astonishing din just over the rise. We stopped, awestruck. It went on for minutes: howling, yapping, shrieking, growling, raging back and forth. We considered retreat, fearing that the ruction was going to sweep over the rise and we would end up in the middle, but slowly it faded into the distance. We figured that coyotes had surprised a large flock of wild turkeys and everyone was in full voice. Being town people, we had never heard anything like this. Next morning we looked for traces of the encounter but found nary a feather nor a snag of fur.

With our dog Sheba we carefully study the scats we find in the fields, in the woods, and on the road. All of us want to know who is visiting our land. We are especially interested in big hairy scats dropped always in the middle of the road. Coyotes are very private and we have seen them only on a few occasions, but they like to give notice of their presence and are bold in leaving signs. For a while we found large piles of fur-filled dung each morning in the middle of our deck. It wasn't a dog or a raccoon, it wasn't a fox or a wolf, so we figured it had to be a coyote neighbor sneaking up at night to squat and drop a sign, giving us the equivalent of the coyote middle finger.

Walking on our road, I once saw a coyote in the distance, trying to hustle some small animal out of its hole, and I was able to watch it through the binoculars. It was intent on its snack, so I had an opportunity to study it carefully. Its head was all ears, eyes, and mouth, amazing alertness—so much depending on it. Its reddish-brown tail twitched and swished as it rooted and pounced.

I found an animal den in the south side woods, a large hollow in the base of a tree with a burrow dug deep into the ground around the roots. I thought it might be for coyotes, but then I smelled the cloying, skunklike odor of a fox. Perhaps they alternate residence. We've seen a fox only once, when we turned a corner in the road and saw his red silhouette in the distance against the green underbrush. We must have been upwind from him and he was intent on hunting, but he ran away as soon as he became aware of us. Richie Halverson suggested that we look for the fox at the same time in the same place the next day. Foxes have regular habits and rounds. We tried to do this, but we aren't quite as well organized as foxes.

Richie told us again recently that he thought he had seen a wolf in the south field between the garden and the Morton building. We found large, fascinating tracks in the upper fields in the snow—but it is hard to tell. There were big pads and claws, a long stride, almost too long for a coyote. But a timber wolf? It was probably a big dog. We have heard no reports of farm animals being attacked. But coyotes, deer, and turkeys are plentiful, and a wolf could live on them for a long time.

I stepped out of the house one autumn day, my mind intent on the work I was going to do in my writing shack. The sky was inky, there was rumbling in the west, and the wind was blowing in on me. As I walked I looked up and saw a blond, shaggy coyote standing by the Morton building with its tail between its legs. It must have been ruminating, too, because it did not see me. Perhaps it was thinking about where it was going to go in the cold downpour. It turned and walked toward me with its head down, still in thought, until finally it became aware of me. Its surprised leap turned it around and it was off in one motion down the hill toward the baring wood. Just before disappearing into the underbrush, it stopped to look back, probably angry with itself for its carelessness.

I was a bit spooked by this encounter. What if it hadn't looked up until it was much closer? What if Sheba had been with me? She is a feisty creature and I have had to separate her from more than one dustup with other dogs. I do not think she would stand well against a coyote—a fight I would not care to have to break up.

Taking a Punch

He can run, but he can't hide.

Joe Louis

My LIFETIME FIGHT RECORD is perfect—one win, no losses. I don't aim to improve it. I was eleven when my parents sent me for a week to the diocesan summer camp near Youngstown, a tidy outpost in the woods and weeds with morning mass, swimming, softball, crafts, and nature hikes. There were a lot of "sponsored" kids from the tough parts of Youngstown, Canton, and Akron, and there was serious combat every day behind the bunkhouses. When I saw blood flowing I kept a very low profile.

The counselors tried to channel the aggression. The tradition at Father Kane's Camp was Friday-night boxing matches. A counselor named Cannonball Kelly was in charge of match-making and scheduling. A burly, sunburned guy with a brown crew cut, he was called Cannonball because he could almost empty the pool with his spectacular belly-smackers off the diving board.

During the week a number of boys asked me if I would box them on Friday night. I knew they had sized me up and were anxious to beat the snot out of me in front of everyone. I had made friends with an older boy from Warren named Francie Wunderly. He was a glib kid, had been to the camp before and knew his way around. We played endless games of mumblety-peg and chattered about the Cleveland Indians. He kept trying to talk me into a match at the fights. From just the usual boyish pull and shove I knew he was much stronger than I, but he kept pestering, giving me reassurances that we would only be sparring around in the ring. He did me a lot of favors and took my part in some squabbles, so finally I agreed. We reported to Cannonball Kelly in the common room to have our match scheduled. There were no scales, but Cannonball picked us each up under our elbows and judged our weight. He sized up my scrawny arms and legs. "You sure you want to do this?" No, I did not want to do it. But Francie was standing there, and so were a lot of other boys. "Sure," I said. "Sure," as ice water flushed the folds of my stomach.

I spent the rest of the week dreading Friday night, but Francie kept reassuring me. "We'll just dance around and put on a show. Maybe I'll take a dive."

Friday night after chow we went to our bunkhouse, put on swim trunks and bathrobes, and went to the common room. The crowd had already gathered. The counselors made a real event of it. They brought wooden benches in from outside and formed them around the ring. Cannonball wore an old tuxedo coat and clip-on black tie. He was the referee and stood in the middle of the ring to bellow out announcements for each match. The matches were three rounds, and Francie and I were fifth on the schedule. As our time approached I quaked down to my small bones. A couple of big kids from Cleveland were the match before ours and I could hear leather smacking on flesh. One kid went down to his knees and Cannonball stepped in to stop it.

My God—we were next! They laced on the big, sweaty gloves and we took our corners. My knees were sapless and palsied. I don't know what was fueling me. Regret and fear. Cannonball announced, "The next match—Francie Wunderly of Warren and Paul Zimmer of Canton. Let's hear it for them!" A light ripple of applause and some guffaws. Older kids were working the corners. My "manager," an older boy from Cleveland, removed my bathrobe and kneaded my bony shoulders as I sat on the stool.

"Hit the fucker in the belly," he advised. "He looks a little soft. Then go upstairs. Tag him. Keep your guard up. Keep ducking and bobbing. Look for an opening." I had forgotten to pee and now I was afraid I might let go. I looked across the ring at Francie and he was staring at me, but then he gave me a little wink and I felt better. Cannonball rang the bell. I got up from the stool and danced tentatively out into the ring.

Francie charged over and whacked me on the side of the head with his right hand. A siren went off in my ear and I almost went down. He came around with his left and caught me in the mouth. I felt my lips crush against my teeth. Then he hit me with his right again hard on the jaw. Comets uncorked in my brain and screwed their tails through my eyeballs, but I stayed on my feet.

Kelly stepped in and pushed Wunderly away, held him at bay until I caught my breath. I wanted to cry, but instead I started shuffling again. Francie walked over and busted me on the cheek. Cannonball reached in and held him off as he looked at me.

"You okay?" he asked.

"Yes," I said and started shuffling again. My voice seemed distant, as if it came from a throat beyond my throat. My vision was clear but objects were remote, as if they existed in some other dimension.

"Keep your guard up!" Kelly said from far away. He released Francie.

The rest of the round Kelly kept bumping Wunderly and staying in his way, so he couldn't get any mustard on his punches. Between rounds Cannonball came over to me. "You can do this," he said. "Keep your guard up and keep moving. You showed him you can take a punch. Now you've got to hit him back. Swing at him. Keep your jab out. He's not that tough. You can *do* it."

He rang the bell again. I stood up and moved a short way off my stool. Francie sprinted across the canvas, starting the punch about midring, and smacked me dead on the nose. Blood spurted onto my chest. As I reeled he charged again and brought his fist up hard into my groin. My vision flashed white, my balls ignited. God, there is no pain like that. I cannot imagine even childbirth or a gunshot wound hurting more. All the savage devils of pain boiled up from my groin, throbbing through intestines and stomach, past my wrenched, astounded heart into my brain, blowing the skullcap off. I howled and bent over. Cannonball raced in and pulled Wunderly off, shouting, "Low blow!" He and my manager helped me to my stool. They wiped the blood off my chest and sponged my face with cold water.

When I could speak, I said, "I can't go anymore." It seemed as if someone in another room was saying this for me.

Cannonball grasped my chin and looked directly into my eyes. "You can do this," he said. "I'm going to end this round now. Only one more to go. I'll keep him off, but you've got to punch. Hit him a few times. Go on. I'm going to give you the fight anyway because of the foul. But you've got to finish it."

I tasted blood and started to cry. From some remote place my voice said, "I want to quit."

"No," Cannonball said. "No, no. Don't cry, Zimmer. Come on. Suck it up."

"I can't do it."

"You can!"

The camp nurse stepped into the ring and came over to look at me. "Maybe you better stop it," she said to Cannonball.

"He can do it," he said. "He needs to do it. I'll help him."

He gave me a few more minutes, then rang the bell again. The boys whooped and hollered, ready for more blood, but the noise seemed to be coming from a football field far away. I stood up and Francie dashed across the ring with his arm cocked, but Cannonball bumped him away and pulled me out to the center. "Arms up, move around," he told me. "*Hit* him!"

Francie was flailing away at me from behind Cannonball's thigh, but I danced back and kept my guard up. Cannonball bumped him again hard with his hip and he stumbled off balance toward me. I swung with my right hand and connected on the side of his neck. Francie looked surprised. It felt good. Before he could react I hit him again on his cheek. The boys cheered and this enraged Francie. He charged at me swinging wildly, but Cannonball caught him and held him up in the air flailing like a turned-over beetle as he signaled for the bell.

He brought us to the center of the ring and held up my right hand, announcing from far away, "The winner by technicality—Paul *Zimmer*. Zimmer!" A few of Francie's friends booed, but most of the boys cheered. By God, it seemed as though somehow, in that other dimension, I *had* won. I had the wit to clasp my gloved hands together and raise them over my head.

For several days Francie tried to act like my friend again, but I wasn't interested. My perceptions remained somewhere in the distance; voices arrived from remote places, until gradually things began to center once more. I realized I had been taught a lesson, but I wasn't certain what I had learned. One thing was for certain, though—I would not fight again. I quit while I was undefeated.

Joe Louis was heavyweight champion through my boyhood, an icon of my youth. I was only three when he won the title from Jim Braddock in 1937, but I was fifteen when he retired in 1949 and I remember most of his fights. He destroyed many white hopes and was "a credit to his race." He defended his title twenty-five times, knocking out twenty-one. He beat the power of Two-Ton Tony Galento, Tami Mauriello, both Baers—Max and Buddy—and he beat the speed of Paulino Uzcuden, Jesse Willard, Tommy Farr, Jersey Joe Walcott, and fast Billy Conn. Quietly and efficiently he knocked most of them cuckoo.

We listened to the fights on the big Philco in our living room. If they came on too late, my parents put me to bed but turned the radio up loud enough so I could hear. I remember my mother laughing at dad when Louis knocked out Buddy Baer. The Baer brothers were formidable specimens physically and verbally. Max had even knocked out the Italian giant Primo Carnera. Buddy Baer had done a lot of talking and convinced many people he would win. My dad for the first time bet against the Brown Bomber. Everyone thought Baer was too big and strong, but Baer went down in a heap in six rounds.

Tami Mauriello came tearing out of his corner at the beginning of his bout with Louis and rocked the Brown Bomber with a couple of heavy punches. The crowd roared and the announcer could barely be heard. Dad sat up on the couch and I danced around the living room with excitement. But Louis sucked it up and finished him off in the first round. When they interviewed Mauriello after the fight the announcer asked, "What happened?"

Into the NBC microphone, to the greater audience of the nation, Mauriello blurted, "I got too God damned careless!"— an utterance that next day became the delighted center of discussion on every grade school playground in the country.

Louis's second fight with Billy Conn was a major media event for the time. I was seven years old when they first fought in 1941 and have little memory of it. Conn, a flashy boxer from Pittsburgh, was a distinct underdog, but he gave Louis fits for fifteen rounds, losing on a very close decision. When they both returned from the service in 1945, a rematch was inevitable and the buildup became intense. No one could match Louis's power, but perhaps craftiness could defeat him. It was power versus speed. It was *Frankenstein Meets the Wolf Man*. The movie had come out a year or so before, and the big question on our playground was whether Frankenstein's power or Wolf Man's speed would triumph. It was on the Catholic Index, so none of us were permitted to go. I own a VCR now and gaze at the movie periodically. The final outcome of the monsters' fight is inconclusive. The villagers dynamite a dam and both of them perish in the flood that destroys the castle. But in 1945 Larry Vignos, small but speedy and tough, claimed that he and his brothers had snuck into the movie. "They fought for three hours," he said. "Frankenstein was kicking his ass, but Wolf Man won in the end. He was too fast."

The evening of the second Louis-Conn match I could barely contain myself. We turned the radio on after supper. Paul Whiteman cut his program short for the bout and concluded by saying, "We're going to switch you now to Madison Square Garden in New York for the heavyweight championship bout. It's going to be quite an evening. Who will win—the Brown Bomber from Detroit or Lightning Billy from Pittsburgh? Stay tuned." The results didn't match the excitement. Conn had lost his edge in the service and went down in eight rounds.

Louis's championship bouts were neighborhood events, and were much discussed. Our neighbor Ron Flynn was a racist bigot. He lost all his bets against Louis and it made him bitter. He uttered terrible things about the champion. "He's going down this time," Flynn would say as he sipped one of his endless cups of coffee. "He's got a glass jaw. Schmeling caught him. He gets hit a few times, he'll quit. You'll see. That's the way it is with shines. They can't beat a good white man." It was fascinating to watch Flynn lose his bets time after time, claiming fix or foul.

In those postwar days, the anxieties of the war had brought neighbors together. They shared happy and sad news, exchanged pots of good soup and fresh-baked pies. We tuned in to the World Series together, and we didn't have to pay lots of money to listen to championship fights. When I was older I prepared neighborhood lotteries for the championship bouts—thirty pieces of paper to be drawn from a hat, each marked for a fighter and a round ("Louis/11," for example). I'd carry the hat full of slips around the block and sell them for a quarter apiece, so the pot would be seven and a half dollars. I'd buy four or five myself. I wanted that pot badly—it would have kept me in Fleers and Topps bubblegum for months—but I always had to hand the dough over to a neighbor.

Louis came out of retirement and fought Rocky Marciano in 1951. He was thirty-seven years old and his powers had diminished, but he needed the money. Young, invincible Marciano knocked him through the ropes in the eighth round. It was terrible to behold. Louis had been Marciano's boyhood hero, and after the fight Rocky wept in his corner. I was a blasé high school junior, but I was stunned that a man as tough as Marciano could weep. I wept, too.

Everyone has a private collection of memories and impressions of Muhammad Ali. His great fights and confrontations with bigotry were unforgettable. Not much more can be said about his courage and irrepressible intelligence, his wit, his marvelous battle plans, his skill and speed, feints and tricks. He could prance and jab, then around some center of tremendous energy and strength suddenly rock and uncoil to throw a devastating flurry of punches from all angles with both hands, rendering his opponent helpless. Everything about his fights has been written and recorded. We remember his dazzling victories. I also recall some of the poundings he took, how he could shake off ferocious blows and go on. He paid a high price for his boxing glory. I treasure a few obscure personal memories of the man.

Ali is in a television commercial, jumping rope with a little girl. As he dances and twirls his rope, he announces that they are going for the world championship of rope skipping. He taunts the little girl as they hop and spin. "I am the greatest!" he shouts. Then suddenly he misses. He drops the rope in despair, shakes his head, and says, "Oh well, at least I'm still the heavyweight champion of the world!"

"Oh yeah!" the little girl shouts, then runs over and belts him on the thigh. Ali reels and falls to the floor.

Ali is on Howard Cosell's television show with Joe Frazier before one of their bouts. Ali is baiting Frazier, who is growing increasingly angry. Finally he stands up and moves menacingly toward Ali. Ali rises and engages him and they wrestle each other to the floor in front of Cosell's desk. Cosell is stunned, doesn't know what to do, and the handlers are cursing and trying to pull them apart. The station cuts to a commercial and I howl with frustration. When they come back on, Ali is sitting in his chair again. Frazier is gone. Cosell says, "Folks, I'm sorry to say Joe Frazier has walked out. Muhammad, do you think he will be coming back?"

"Naw, he won't be coming back."

"Why did you guys do that?"

"The man stood up and moved toward me. What was I supposed to do?"

"Why did he do that?"

"His feelings were hurt," Ali said, studying a small cut on his hand. "He's very sensitive."

Norman Mailer is in Zaire to write about Ali's "Rumble in the Jungle" with George Foreman. Mailer jogs on the road into the jungle every morning for some showy exercise. Ali and his handler, Bundhini Brown, get a tape recording of a lion roaring and set it up in the jungle just off the road. They stretch out on the hotel porch as Mailer bounces out in his sweats. "Mornin', Noh-man." When he runs down the road a ways they trip the tape on loud with a remote control. Mailer comes barreling back as if pursued by the Simba devil.

Ali, in Germany for a fight with Carl Mildenberger, is being interviewed by Cosell. There are some German children in the background and Ali is mugging and feinting punches with them. Cosell, baiting Ali, asks why he has come all the way to Germany to fight a second-rate fighter. Ali says, "Why are you putting that on me, Howard? What are you complaining about? I got you a trip to a beautiful place. Here we are with these nice people. You're eating potato pancakes and schnitzel in good restaurants. If it weren't for me you'd be back in New York getting mugged and dodging taxis."

Then there is the heartbreaking, incredibly moving scene at the 1996 Olympic games when Ali lights the Olympic fire with the torch handed to him by the runner. This brave, effervescent, powerful man, who first gained notice in the Olympic games, now walks with a hobble and cannot speak clearly. But he is smiling, and we are all happy for him. A friend of mine once commented, "The only problem with Ali was that he could take a punch." He took many from his powerful opponents, more than he should have, more than he needed to—but perhaps not more than we wanted him to. He represented some of us. We watched it all.

We had a Friday-night ritual at our house. My folks savored a Manhattan because it was the end of the week, although they both had to go to work on Saturday. Then we had fish for dinner and a game of canasta. Just before eight o'clock my mom took her book upstairs, I threw some pillows on the floor, and my dad plunked down on the couch.

It was time for the *Friday Night Fights.* We listened on the big radio to Don Dumphy give his rat-a-tat, blow-by-blow descriptions while Bill Corum provided commentary between the rounds. We heard the matches of Fritzie Zivic, Tony Janiero, Gus Lesnevich, Archie Moore, Beau Jack, Chalky Wright, Marcel Cerdan, Gene Fullmer, Ike Williams, Jake LaMotta, the great exchange of championship bouts between Rocky Graziano and Tony Zale, Willie Pepp and Sandy Saddler. When we got television in the early 1950s we watched the fights of Kid Gavilan, Irish Bob Murphy, Bobo Olson, Sugar Ray Robinson, Ezzard Charles, Jersey Joe Walcott, Carmen Basilio. We both fancied we were good judges of pugilists and worked up dime bets on the matches. My dad liked a muscular heavyweight named Bob Satterfield, who looked great and started fast but usually ended in a bloody heap on the canvas. When Satterfield fought I knew I was into Cracker Jack for the week. After the fights, inspired by what we had seen, my dad and I sparred a little in the living room on the way to bed until mom called down for us to desist.

Years later I watched the fights with my son. The bets had gone up to a dollar and Erik won a lot more than I did. There is no question that we found them interesting and exciting. Did we enjoy seeing men hammer each other senseless? I guess we did. I console myself by thinking that we also appreciated bravery, skill, conditioning, control, and the gathering of power into crucial moments.

But I have seen terrible things in boxing matches. I watched horrified as George Foreman knocked Joe Frazier down three times in the second round of their bout. The tough Frazier, knocked senseless, still got up, only to be blasted down once more, his head going back and forth like a bruised apple in high wind. I was screaming at the television screen, "Stop it! Stop it!" I did the same thing as I watched Ingemar Johansson punching Floyd Patterson's head in their first bout, and when Rocky Marciano was blasting Joe Louis through the ropes. I watched some of Mike Tyson's various slaughters, fascinated and appalled at how he has embodied violence, like a grenade with its pin pulled. I have seen two deaths in the ring—a furious Emil Griffith punching Benny Kid Paret to death, and Boom Boom Mancini's lethal fight with the Korean fighter Du Koo Kim. These things were hideous.

Stop it! Stop it! I know what it means to be knocked into the funny room. Even little boys can do it. Why do we watch? Tough guys going down to tough guys. These are the stallions. When the action becomes furious, that's when we become most excited. Do the fighters stand for us? Most of us are not stallions. The thrill is vicarious and the great battlers signify us, as ancient men identified with their champions. They become our metaphor.

But we have come a long way from that kind of representative anarchy. We are controlled, generally pacific creatures in the conduct of our daily lives. This is civilization. We do violence with our tongues, with our words in memos and in secret meetings; we can even do damage with the touch of a "send" button, but we suppress the desire to physically crunch our enemies. Crimes are committed and news is made when we are unable to restrain these impulses. Violence and misbehavior, controlled or uncontrolled, interest us. The entertainment and sports industries bank big money on this. Stallions and mares are paid to do—or pretend to do—violence for us. We come home from our little lives of quiet desperation and switch it on.

Women now box professionally, and they bang on each others' faces and breasts. I am just hypocritical enough to switch these matches off. I cannot watch them. I do not care who reminds me of my double-mindedness. But everyone has a right to violent representatives.

Now boxing seems almost genteel and passé as interest swings to "ultimate fighting," and real bar fighters are paid to bloody each other in public. Professional wrestling is all connotation, a theater of absurd violence, a tawdry imitation of cruelty. These are the gods and devils pretending to hammer on each other, the bad people versus the good. So few of us could be that powerful—but the violence, even if it is play-acting and tumbling, somehow represents us. Arthur Koestler once suggested that if the human race is to survive it will have to be tranquilized en masse.

As a boy I staged battles and violently banged my lead soldiers together in combat until their limbs or heads would break off. I cut out pictures of football players and boxers, made up games for them, and slashed them together until they were shreds. Now this is done for young people in video games. If you have enough quarters you can blow up the world. I stepped into a video parlor once and studied the players, young and old. They all looked like mad bombers in the flickering lights of the machines.

Would I explode and commit violence if my aggressive feelings were not represented for me in some way? I have many gentle friends who watch no violent sports or entertainment. I go for months without watching boxing. But when I turn it on I watch it as I would a frightening murder mystery or a candid love scene in a movie. It manifests part of my nature. I am not prurient, but I sure as hell am readily interested.

As a birthday treat for Erik, when he was a boy, several times I took him and a group of his friends to the Golden Gloves regional championship bouts in Pittsburgh. The lads were fascinated. Pittsburgh is a tough town. Walking into that atmosphere was like stepping into Casimir's mead hall. The crowd was peppered with old fighters and street people. Draft Iron City flowed freely. Everyone had loud advice for the pugilists. At times the fights in the crowd were more interesting than the ones in the ring. The card of three-round bouts was long and the evening extended. It grew late and we usually had to leave before the heavyweights came on, to the great disappointment of the boys.

One of Erik's friends had a gymnasium set up in the basement of his house. The boys decided to arrange their own card of fights. For weeks they went to this basement after school, put on their swim trunks, and trained for matches, shadowboxing, skipping rope, sparring, and punching the bags. Erik asked his mother to serve him steak every night, and he reported the training activities at dinner.

Each fighter had a trainer; talk was thick as the baby palookas taunted each other. Erik was going to knock his opponent out. He wouldn't predict his round, but the kid was going to go down. He spent most of his time slugging the heavy bag. He shadowboxed in front of the mirror in his room before leaving for school. They terrorized each other with their boasts. Excitement mounted as the scheduled day approached and the bluster grew thicker. Erik began to grow uneasy and quiet. I could tell he was worried. The kid he was fighting was bigger and plenty tough. I recalled Francie Wunderly all those years ago and started worrying myself. I began to feel guilty. I bought Erik a mouthpiece and a jock strap. I suspect some of the parents were not happy with me for taking the boys to the Golden Gloves matches, and I admit to some regret myself. Erik said an older high school boy was going to referee. I thought about calling him but decided not to intrude. Some of the children from school were invited to the gym to act as the crowd. There was much discussion about whether to charge admission.

The morning of the great Saturday fights somebody begged off because he was sick, then another called to say he had misbehaved and had to stay home as punishment. Still another boy wasn't sure he could fight because he had banged his knee. Then the whole card crumbled and the combatants all went off together to see a science fiction movie. I admit feeling considerable relief. Civilization reigned. I breathed easily again. I did not want my son to be taking punches or representing my aggressions.

It was the middle of a difficult week. Suzanne had taken her book to bed and I threw cushions on the floor and plopped down to watch *Top Rank Boxing,* a weekly traveling show of bouts between "up and coming" professional fighters from boxing outposts like St. Paul, Biloxi, Gary, Knoxville, Portland, Fort Worth. The cards and quality of boxing were uneven, but sometimes the main bout was worth watching. Because I was tired I decided to watch the preliminary bouts as well. The second three-rounder featured a couple of tough, active black middleweights who didn't like each other. They had a cold, intimidating staring match at the instructions and when they came out at the bell there was no exploratory sparring; they were immediately on each other, pounding and loading up their punches. They taunted each other as they grappled. By the third round many hard blows had been landed and they were both badly beaten up, their eyes and jaws swollen, bleeding cuts spattering the canvas.

Just as Suzanne walked into the room to get a magazine, one fighter connected with a bone-jarring uppercut, then pounded his opponent's head back and forth with a vicious combination of punches. The man fell back into a corner and the aggressor charged in to lean against him, prop him up against the ropes, and pound his midsection, then delivered three straight hard shots to the head before the referee was able to pull him off. The beaten man slithered sickeningly down the ropes to a sitting position on the canvas, then fell over. His eyes were crossed and his arms and legs were quaking.

Suzanne cried out. My hair stood on end. The other fighter was still trying to get at his stricken opponent as the referee held him back. Trainers swarmed into the ring. The fight doctor was already down on his hands and knees over the beaten fighter. Suzanne was weeping. "My God! How can you watch that?"

I felt stupid and guilty. "I didn't know it was going to happen."

"Awful! That's awful." She stormed from the room. I could hear her sobbing as she walked down the hall. The cameras moved away from the downed fighter and showed the winner waving his arms in jubilation as he was borne victoriously around the ring.

Then everyone was waiting. The camera stayed off the beaten man. The television commentators pattered as the camera panned the quiet, serious faces in the crowd. The ring announcer paced the canvas, talking nervously to the referee and handlers. There were two commercials, but when the program returned to the arena everything was still in quiet suspension. Then you could tell that they had brought in a stretcher. Even the television guys shut up. The cameras didn't show it, but all eyes in the crowd watched as the young man was hustled up the aisle and out of the arena. Finally the announcers admitted that the beaten fighter seemed to be "having a bit of difficulty." They spoke glibly of the risks in the ring. The ring announcer held up the arm of the now solemn victor, and the camera swung to the two commentators, who began jabbering about the upcoming main event.

I stayed with it through the announcement and instructions, watched until the fighters exchanged initial blows, then shut the television off, gazing at the light of the screen as it became a line, then gathered into a bright spot in the center before fading away.

Suzanne was still reading when I went into the bedroom. I knew she didn't want to talk, but I tried to say a few things to explain myself. My voice seemed remote, as if it was coming from another room. She did not respond. I went into the bathroom with my pajamas and took a shower. When I came out she had switched off the light and turned on her side away from me.

Deer

In the autumn mating season the male deer fight. We find bits of shattered antlers in the woods and violent scuffle marks in the frosted grass of the fields. But we find gentler signs as well. Deer are a constant presence; silent and elegant, they munch and stroll in the fields. We saw them on our first walk at twilight, five shadowy figures at the bottom of the sloped field, their heads raised from grazing. I held Wanda, our Great Dane, by the collar, but she didn't strain, apparently as surprised and fascinated as we were. The deer watched us, standing stock-still for several minutes in their places. Then the largest snorted and they all bounded away into the woods, their white tails flicking like ostrich feathers in the fading light.

Next morning as I headed for my writing shack, they were in the same place, their heads straight up, watching me for some moments before disappearing into the trees. They are our wary neighbors; seeing them is part of our lives, part of our precious silence.

Occasionally we come across places where deer have lain, usually in grassy places just off the edge of the fields, but often we find hollows in the tall grass or snow in the middle of fields, where they have stretched out head to head. Sometimes when it is cold these places still hold warmth and I imagine their winter coats tipped with frost, spirits of their breath rising in the chill as they lie together. Like the ghosts of dead friends, not wishing to disturb or be disturbed, they move on when they hear us coming, leaving behind the smell of musk and sweat.

We find deer bones in the woods, sometimes skulls with racks, long snouts with sharply chiseled nostrils, and huge, grinding teeth. I wedge them in the crotches of trees and we visit them in our walks to witness how the antlers are whittled away by birds or insects that need their calcium.

On a November day as we were getting the first flurries of the year, we saw a yearling doe bound out of the woods, prancing in the fields with great excitement. It was her first snow, and so she skittered and zigzagged in wonder, flicking her snout at the flakes. We realized that she was playing—there was no other word for it. We felt kinship, remembered doing the same thing in first snows when we were children, dashing about and sticking our tongues out to catch the flakes.

Deer scourge the young saplings and gorge on Richie's corn and oats, sometimes munch on our garden and chew the tops off young evergreens I plant, but they are our dignified neighbors. I wish I could hold my head that high, wish I could become airborne and sleek, bound through the trees and dash into meadows with unconstrained wildness.

Brown is not one of my favorite colors, but the tan coats of deer, when they stand in sunlight, enthrall me—they are luminous, liquid, and beautiful. I watched a fawn near my writing shack through field glasses, walking toward me as if it were going to come right into the room. Sheba was dozing quietly on her rug, so the fawn came all the way up to stand by my window, unaware of our presence. I gazed at its coppery coat and white spots, its small, muscular body, the young head and very large eyes, and felt privileged.

The Hunt

W E ALWAYS KNOW when the war with animals is about to begin. In October nights we see bright lights in the fields and sweeping flashes in the valleys and on the ridges—hunters, in their pickups with swivel-beam lights on their cabs, looking for feeding deer. It is called spotting; the hunters are locating the herd.

We post our land with NO HUNTING signs (I even have one that says CHASSE INTERDIT) and allow only Richie Halverson to bring in a small party on opening day in November. It is always the same. We are awakened again by distant gunfire. I throw the curtain in our bedroom and far down the road on the rise are three figures clad in absurd red-orange suits, standing on the horizon, their pickups parked near the old pump. Later two more trucks arrive, and last year there were eight hunters, pointing and talking, and a small boy with a BB gun. The party included Richie and his son, Will Cobble and his two sons, Richie's other brother-in-law and his brother-in-law's brother. I don't know who the other two were. The little boy was Richie's grandson. I looked at them through the field glasses. They were drinking coffee out of thermoses, cradling high-powered rifles in the crooks of their arms, and surveying the fields below.

Richie Halverson is master of the hunt. He had agreed with
me that there would be only five hunters on my land. He is a
friendly, accommodating man, so I figure things got away from
him. Nevertheless, I am angry. Richie has hunted this land, as
did his father and grandfather, since he was a small boy. I own
the land, but on opening day all bets are off. I am the permanent visitor, to be tolerated and educated, if possible; but
opening day is ancient ritual and strangers have no real part in
it. If I wanted to, I would be permitted to join the hunting
party. They look upon our land as prime grounds. There are
ridges and slopes to sight down all the way to the trees. They
always begin here at dawn on opening day, scanning from the
top of our ridge, then later in the day they drift off to hunt
their own lands.

If I told Richie I wanted no hunting on my land, he would
honor my wishes, but then I would really become a discourte-
ous, boorish alien. He has already put a small freeze on me for
signing our fields into a set-aside program. The life of a small
dairy farmer is difficult; the work is all-consuming, exhausting
routine. Hunting is a reward for the long, mindless job of
milking the herd, for growing and harvesting hay through the
heat of the summer. I try very hard to keep this in mind,
remembering that my permission to hunt is a way for me to
participate in the community.

Richie checks our property when we are absent and makes
certain no other hunters trespass. This is his exchange for the
hunting. He always thanks me most courteously when the season is over. Will Cobble dumps a pickup load of firewood
outside the Morton building every few years, and this is his
trade for the hunting.

They used to gut their slain deer and leave the offal in the
fields for carrion birds and coyotes. The stomachs were large
wine-colored bags full of half-digested corn and grass. Our
dog Wanda loved to come across these and gorge herself, then

she would be sick for a couple of days. So one of our unfailing rules is that the hunters carry garbage bags and haul the viscera away.

For the first few days of deer hunting season we are displaced on our own land and dare not set out on our morning walk with the dog. I am even reluctant to go down the road to my writing shack. Hell, those are guns out there—with *bullets* in them! Indeed, Richie's brother-in-law usually sits in his bright suit, cradling his rifle, on the bench outside the shack. Our first year on the place I had the temerity to walk out for my morning writing session. I chatted briefly with the brother-in-law, then went into the shack. I knew he was curious about what I was doing in there, but I was also wondering how he could possibly enjoy sitting out in the cold in that silly, blazing jumpsuit. I worked at my poems inside, and he held his post outside with his rifle at the ready, as if he were a sentry for the muse.

When I finished writing, I walked out on the ridge to see what was happening. Richie was sitting in his pickup with the engine running when I came up. He was very friendly, but I realized he was studying me carefully. Then I saw in the bed of his truck a young two-point buck lying on its side. It had been gutted and blood ran down the ridges of the rubber mat. Its eyes were open and still held the sheen of surprise and fear. The vibration of the idling truck made its fur seem to stir. Richie could tell I was bothered because he said, "He's young. He'll be good eating." He was either trying to justify the killing or straighten me out about hunting. Perhaps both.

Later that day at twilight, after the hunt, we looked out the bedroom window and a young deer slowly crossed the road, pondering and sniffing. Suzanne imagined it might be the sibling of the deer that had been killed, looking for its missing brother. As we gazed at the deer in silhouette, she quietly asked me if I could tell the difference in that half light between the deer and our Great Dane, Wanda. I admitted that if I were a young man with buck fever I might not take the time to see the disparity.

I watch the hunters and hear them shooting deer on my property. I have seen them charge down a slope, firing away like an infantry squad at some hapless, bounding animal zigzagging, trying to head for the trees, already faltering and stumbling from a ferocious wound until it collapses. I hate it. It appalls me.

I am an alien in hunting season—a displaced person. It is as if I stumble into a war zone, another world that does not care for or value what I am. The past and future mean nothing; only the present is vital. My communicative skills become useless; any prerogative I have has been eroded.

One November day I stopped at a small station in Gays Mills to buy gasoline. The attendant came out and pumped my fuel, then I made the mistake of following him into the station to get my change. It was filled with hunters swigging ritual cans of beer, some of them stripped down to their T-shirts, leaning on pop coolers and sitting on oily benches. A few of them had blackened their faces. The place smelled like a Viking hall. A hunter was telling a story, pointing to a place on his chest just in front of his armpit. "Right here's where it went in," he said, "but that sucker kept on going. Tracked it most of a morning till I found it."

The talk stopped when they realized I had come into their presence. I was on my way to our farm from a week of work at my office, and I had not removed my tie and coat. I felt as if I had wandered in from another planet. Their looks were cold and suspicious. These were men I would have chatted with pleasantly on the street, but in this season and in this place they were bonded and transformed. No matter who I was or what I had been, dressed as I was, I had nothing to say to them under these conditions, and they resented my presence. The attendant hurried with my change.

I doubt that I will ever grow accustomed to hunting season. I know we must "thin the herd," the old must make way for the young, the weakened and worn for the strong. I know our species was able to evolve because of hunting. I recognize it as ancient ritual. The first primitive poets were probably raconteurs of the hunt. I do not hesitate to eat the flesh of animals. But I will never get used to seeing these magnificent creatures being hounded and cruelly slaughtered, proudly displayed as victims, strapped across the hoods of trucks, and stacked in pickup beds like cordwood. Their stiffened bodies are thrown into piles in the cold lockers of local butchers to be cut up, and mostly ground into sausage. They are strung up from trees en masse, on display like the dead enemies of Caesar in front yards, their tongues lolling out and blood dripping into the grass from their orifices. One almost expects to see them surrounded by leering lynch mobs.

As a young man I learned an emphatic lesson: never trust brutality as representative of anything worthy. Yet I admit to my fascination with war stories, boxing, and football. Violence is part of my human heritage, but I know it does not enduringly signify superiority, prestige, manhood, or humanity. When it prevails, our species is sullied and diminished.

The Blind World

*Behold, all ye that kindle a fire, that compass yourselves about
with sparks: walk in the light of your fire, and in the sparks that
ye have kindled. This shall ye have of mine hand; ye shall lie
down in sorrow.*

Isaiah 50:11

I HAVE A 1955 SNAPSHOT of myself that always amazes
people. A private (E2) in the U.S. Army, I am standing in the
desert. I have a pencil in my shirt pocket and the flap is open.
Probably there are poems scribbled on folded papers in that
pocket. My shoes are unshined, my fatigues rumpled. Just off
my right elbow, from behind a mountain, the mushroom of an
atomic explosion is lifting into blue sky as leisurely as a cumulus cloud. It rises above my head, soaring in its power. I am
callow, slender, smiling my snapshot smile as if I'm vacation-
ing on a sandy beach.

In fact, I was just a boy, and it *was* a kind of vacation day
for all of us. Normally all the men in my unit were moved out
into the desert as ground observers for the detonations, but
this was a small, daytime test—near enough so we could witness it from our camp. The army was not participating in the

field. There were just four of us in the office that day. The rest of the staff members were out on assignments. We were told to stay inside tents or buildings until after the flash, when we could walk out to observe.

By then we had already witnessed a half dozen tests. This one seemed almost casual. We went on duty that morning, made coffee at ten o'clock. At eleven, as we worked, the walls and ceiling, the papers on our desks, even the keys on our typewriter boards brightened suddenly. We tucked our heads down instinctively and waited until the shock rumbled over the tin roof of our office, then stepped outside. The head clerk brought out his camera and snapped our pictures as we posed beside the distant mushroom cloud. Then I took his picture. We stood together chatting, gazing at the mushroom cloud as it began to drift in the morning sky. Looking at my photo recently I noticed, after all the years, a rather large swelling on my left hand. I have a dim recollection of being alarmed by this curious budding, but I was ingenuous and indestructible; I ignored it, like most maladies of young manhood, until it went away.

This was the middle of the 1950s. The Allies had won the Second World War a decade before, ending it with the world's first atomic bombs, and now America was preparing to defend itself against other enemies. We had just fought a bloody police action in Korea, but the next war was likely to be even more brutal and definitive. Our government was trying to learn how to sustain at least a portion of its armed forces while the destruction would be occurring. They were blowing up atolls in the Pacific as sailors witnessed and their ships rocked on tidal waves. This is why our small group of army personnel was assigned to maneuvers in Nevada while the Atomic Energy Commission tested bombs there in the desert.

The army participants were the only living creatures in the immediate blast area besides the penned animals and creatures of the desert. We were called "atomic guinea pigs" by the news media. The expressed official purpose of our presence in the exercises was to allow the military to show that troops could be indoctrinated in methods and strategies of atomic warfare, and to measure the psychological effects of an atomic explosion on soldiers.

I don't know what they were really expecting from us, but we were uniformly scared out of our minds. We cringed in the bottom of slit trenches; had we stood up we would have been blown down, maimed and burned, either dead or cruelly wounded, of no military use at all. I don't recall ever being observed or questioned about how I felt. The officers must have been dealing with their own trauma.

I was twenty years old. We were all young, a broad mix of men assembled from every section of the country. We were given only minimal information. There were times when we were terrified speechless. Such conditions sustain brotherhood: after duty hours in camp we sorted ourselves out by race, education, area, and background, but we stuck together in common apprehension.

It was in this violent place that I firmly decided I wanted to be a poet, but my flight was not exactly that of the phoenix. Forty-five years have passed. In some ways those mushroom clouds have been ascending ever since. Whenever I come across my photograph, I remember this story.

Camp Desert Rock was rows and rows of dusty olive tents where enlisted men slept. There was an area of rough wooden barracks nailed up in the center for officer quarters and base offices. The brigadier general in command was quartered in a khaki house trailer on the edge of the encampment. The latrines, showers, supply section, and infirmary were in corrugated steel buildings. The best building was an officers' club, constructed by the engineers so the brass could belly up every night. The post exchange was a Quonset hut with a few picnic tables for beer drinking. A single airstrip accommodated small craft. Visiting generals arrived here, jumping out of helicopters like linebackers.

I worked in public information, housed in a larger shack with a kerosene heater. I shuffled papers, did typing, and composed little prescripted stories for hometown newspapers about guys who were in the atomic maneuvers. When the officers and head clerk were out of the office, I worked on my poems unless I was assigned to coordinate visits by civilian reporters, who wanted to get in and out of the place as fast as possible.

It was dusty and cold in those winter months on the desert. Yucca Flat was sand, scrub, and long, straight dirt roads. There were dismal gray-brown foothills in the distance, a few of them high enough to bear patches of snow. The regular army noncoms said it reminded them of Korea. Wind blew all the time, making our teeth gritty and caking our nostrils with sand. Our eyeballs felt as if they were rolling on sandpaper. While I was there, two violent windstorms blew down all the tents in camp.

The civilian photographers and reporters all wanted to know where to go and which way to point their cameras so they could get pictures of mushroom clouds. We were a big story in the midfifties. Once, newsman John Cameron Swayze showed up at our office with a television crew. Dave Garroway, host of the *Today Show*, walked in one cold day—aloof, imperious, deliberate—wearing a big overcoat and knocking everyone out with his presence. I was smoking a cigarette and became the office hero for a week when Garroway bummed one.

Celebrities are part of the coin in the Las Vegas area. In the fifties people still felt patriotic about soldiers. No tests were conducted on weekends, and things were slow in the casinos, so the hotel owners sometimes sent their shows out to Desert

Rock on Sunday afternoons to entertain the troops. Marie Wilson, Vaughn Monroe, and Gypsy Rose Lee came with small bands and magnificent chorus girls who bumped into each other as they giggled and pranced on our little Quonset-hut stage.

In 1955 the army participated in eight tests, including one midair explosion and an underground one. Some bombs were detonated from towers; others were dropped from airplanes. We were never told how far our trenches were from ground zero.

I've thought often about those experiences—this massive threat to humanity we were compelled to witness as very young men. Sometimes the visions return to me in bad dreams. The government told us we were modern heroes; we were featured in newspapers and newsreels. Officers told us we were making history, were doing the most important thing we would ever do in our lives. We were given a booklet that said, "You can remember with a sense of pleasure and accomplishment that you were a real pioneer in experimentation of the most vital importance in the security of the United States."

They told us almost nothing about radiation. If it was mentioned, our officers dismissed it as an "overrated thing." The booklet instructed us to "maintain security discipline." It included warnings about health hazards—not from radiation but from "the indigenous reptiles and poisonous insects of the desert." Buses that moved us to the forward area were equipped with two brooms clamped just outside the doors. After witnessing a test and before reboarding, we were required to whisk each other off; then we held our arms out away from our bodies while a radiological safety man ran a handheld Geiger counter over us.

The final reading on the film badge I wore throughout my time at Desert Rock (measuring my cumulative radiation exposure) was never revealed to me. Years later when I inquired of the Department of the Army, they told me the records had perished in a fire in a government office building in Kansas City.

When I arrived in Nevada—at the Las Vegas Union Railroad Station at 3:00 A.M.—no connecting limousines were running, so I had to take a cab to the bus depot. Las Vegas overwhelmed me as I rode across town. Even in the midfifties it was dazzling with neon, and people were wandering the streets in the wee hours. I got off at the depot, hauled my duffel bag inside, and dropped down on the old, hacked-up wooden benches. The place smelled of Lysol and stale popcorn. The only other people in the waiting room were two drunks sleeping on the slatted seats and a black soldier playing slot machines.

The soldier was bulky and tough looking, but when he saw my uniform he smiled, pocketed his change, and came over. "Hey, man. You coming into Desert Rock?" It was the first time I'd heard the place named out loud. I was keenly aware that I'd been assigned to the atomic testing grounds, but up to then Camp Desert Rock had been obscure, vaguely menacing words printed in the orders I was carrying.

I was a small-city kid from Ohio and hadn't spent much time with black men. I'd been a catcher on a baseball team one summer with a black shortstop and left fielder, but they hung out together and I never really got to know them. I wasn't wary of this man, but I was uncertain. He seemed friendly and genuine, but he watched me carefully, too.

It turned out that he was on a day pass from Desert Rock. His name was Solomon Womble, and he was from Cleveland, only about fifty miles from my hometown of Canton. He sat down beside me and looked up at the clock in the depot. "The ride to Desert Rock don't run till eight in the morning," he said. "You don't want to be in too much of a hurry to get out there anyway." He had a large, very round head, with a scar through one eyebrow, and he sported just a trace of a mustache. He pulled out a pack of Lucky Strikes and offered one. It was the first time a black person had offered me something. I took a cigarette and he snapped open his Zippo for me, then lighted his own.

"We got a long night," Womble said. "Want to try the town? Might as well kill some time. Stash your duffel in one of those lockers and let's get out of here. We can get something to eat, maybe a few free gins if we play the slots a little."

We walked the downtown, buzzing some of the smaller casinos. I was uneasy in this atmosphere, but Womble knew his way around. On the street even the drugstores were open. Nobody seemed the least bit sleepy. That time of night, mostly shadow figures and losers were playing downtown. We had cheese omelettes and steak at a diner, then hoofed it all the way out to the Strip.

In the fifties the Sands was the brightest and gaudiest casino, so we went there first. People were coming and going as if it were a cathedral, a fancier crowd than the one downtown, sober and studied about their playing, hovering over the dollar slots and rolling the bones on those big tables.

The dealers were all friendly and encouraging. People played and played. There was a lot of bravado. Some even tried to pretend they were laughing as they lost, but it was a bad act. They looked so straight and regular, just like folks from my hometown. Womble and I strolled among the tables. Once in a while we'd drop a quarter and yank down the lever on a slot machine, watching the fruits line up. Mostly we looked. The women were glorious, even at five in the morning—the most beautiful I had ever seen.

I didn't see Womble a lot at first after I reported to Desert Rock. Mostly he hung out with the few other black men. But whenever we saw each other, it was, "Hey, man!" and we'd go off for beer in the post exchange. I don't remember what we talked about, probably jazz and women and the Cleveland Indians. We got to be friends—not best buddies, but two guys who appreciated each other. Lonely and young, I recognized his experience and would have tried to strengthen the bond, but Womble knew what was possible. We had some good times. I felt lucky to know him.

After duty hours in the camp, men gathered in groups— the college boys in a tent, Southerners in a corner of the PX beer hall. The noncoms stayed in the mess hall after dinner and spiked their coffee while the KPs cleaned up. Womble and his buddies staked out an area beside the shower Quonset. Sometimes I'd go there to find Womble and was allowed to stay because I knew him. They had propped up some broken mess-hall benches, then sat around and gassed with each other, burning old boards and desert brush in a ten-gallon drum. They'd pass wine, and after a while a few of them would croon rhythm and blues. Womble sang jazz tunes. He had a good, big voice and made a production number out of "Gee, Baby, Ain't I Good to You," which we all admired.

Once, emboldened by a canteen cup full of Thunderbird, I had the temerity to attempt a song. I don't remember what it was—some jazz tune like "Honeysuckle Rose" or "How High the Moon." I closed my eyes when I sang, and when I opened them, they were all looking at me. Mercifully, they hadn't started laughing. Before they could, Womble said emphatically, "That was real good, Zimmer!" That took care of things, but I did not sing again.

Womble did memorable, surprising things. Once he was standing in the chow line and a white guy got into a ruckus with him. There was a lot of pushing and shoving, and everyone got excited. The ugly, electric words were flying. *Jigaboo. Nigger.*

Men started gathering in tense groups. The white guy picked up a big rock and stood ready to crack Womble's head with it.

I remember wanting to go to Womble's aid, to protect him somehow, but he needed no help. He was on the man with astonishing speed, wrapping him round with his powerful arms as the rock rolled away in the sand. Womble bear-hugged him, kicking and hollering, until the sergeants got there and put a stop to it before anything more happened. With one quick move Womble had saved everyone a bloody mess. Later the white guy apologized to him.

Because I was with public information I could float on maneuvers, so I usually arranged to be with Womble's platoon when we went out for a test. I was so brainwashed and indomitable in my seedtime that initially it didn't occur to me that our superiors would expose us to real danger. I realized that these exercises were more threatening than a rifle range, of course, but despite their immensity, I believed we were in safe hands—at least at first, when the bombs were smaller.

But Womble had already seen violence and death in the streets of Cleveland. He recognized danger when he saw it and knew enough to be frightened. He had built up a formidable shell of ghetto toughness, yet the tolerance and gentleness he displayed with me betrayed his sensitivity. Observing him, his wariness and suspicion, made me realize that we were in harm's way. When Womble and I cowered beside each other in the bottom of those trenches during test shots, destruction and death were mere inches over our heads. That is a very serious kind of togetherness.

Once, when we'd been ordered out of our trenches after a detonation, Womble did something that I've never forgotten. We were moving toward the mushroom cloud when someone flushed a jackrabbit, blinded and burned by the flash. It dashed around haplessly, bumping into guys, stumbling over plants and roots. Not surprisingly, some of the men laughed at its pathetic scrambling. Not Womble. When the rabbit collapsed, heaving, resigned to death, Womble approached it and kicked it hard, like a football, end over end through the air. At first I was appalled by this violence. The rabbit was still quivering when it landed, so Womble cracked its head with a rock and then dragged it by a leg under tall yucca. He scraped and dug with his boot heel to make a hole, gently laid the rabbit in, and with his gloved hand covered it with sand. Then he stood up and looked around at us. We looked down and then moved on.

Over tall cans of Regal Pale in the beer hall once, Womble told me that he planned to go to college on the GI Bill. I asked him what he planned to study. "Psychology," he said. "I can usually figure people out. I'm good at it."

I made the decision that I wanted to try to be a poet while I was at Desert Rock—the unlikeliest place to make such a life decision, but I have been happy about it ever since. The drill in camp was tedious when the bombs weren't going off. We were always working and waiting for the next shot, and there wasn't much to do off duty in that bare place. I quickly became bored with sitting in the beer hall. Movies were shown a couple of times a week, but I could take in only so many Doris Day or Piper Laurie films.

By accident I discovered I liked to read books, and in those days you could buy literature in drugstores. I studied the racks in Las Vegas and purchased paperbacks. I made some lucky choices to start with—Hemingway, Thomas Wolfe, Fitzgerald, Carson McCullers, Steinbeck, Salinger. I'd buy a quart of beer every night and lie in my bunk, sipping and reading.

Cleaning tents in the desert is a ridiculous exercise, but I made a life discovery when I was assigned barracks duty. I would beat the canvas sides with a broom, swipe at the dust on the footlockers with a khaki cloth, then sit down for a while and watch the dust settle again. I noticed a paperback book under a bunk. It was *The Pocket Book of Modern Verse.* The subtitle read, "English and American Poetry of the Last 100 Years from Walt Whitman to Dylan Thomas. An Anthology Edited by Oscar Williams."

I still have that book, browning and crumbling in a polyethylene envelope. I will never throw it away. It is the only book I ever stole. I spent the rest of the day with it, and many, many nights thereafter. Someone had written a gin rummy score in green ink on the first page. The names are Mintz and Sacata. I love those guys, whoever they are or were. They did not want this book. Neither Mintz nor Sacata was ever going to be a poet. I was. There, by the grace of some god, in the center of the inferno, I decided I wanted to be a poet.

After a test we would come back in the morning, exhausted by tension and sleeplessness, everyone around me crashing into their bunks fully clothed. But I would sit on my footlocker for a while and read poems. No one stayed awake long enough to make fun of me. I was weary unto death myself, but this seemed a good thing to do after such horribly inarticulate experiences—to touch the most articulate. In this way I preserved my spirit.

Sometimes now I take the Oscar Williams anthology out of its envelope and lovingly turn its browned pages, remembering that early wonder and pleasure. I still enjoy looking at the photographs of the poets. The powerful faces of Whitman, Yeats, Frost, Auden, Millay, and Thomas on the Cardinal Giant cover. Housman, Dickinson, Hardy, Hopkins, cummings, Crane, William Carlos Williams, even Oscar Williams himself on the back. I read again the poems that so enchanted and mystified me. I love this book. Even as it crumbles away, I know it saved my mind and my life.

I was going to be a poet. I bought a Kaywoodie pipe and a can of Sir Walter Raleigh tobacco in the PX, found an old tweed jacket in a St. Vincent de Paul store in Vegas. I told everyone but the sergeants about my plan. I even told Womble. He pondered for a while, then said, "That'd be real good." It took a lot longer than I imagined, but I never looked back.

Out on Yucca Flats the Atomic Energy Commission had a big crew that set the stage for the tests. They built small towns of two-story houses in the desert, painted them up, and placed mannequins in them—mothers in the kitchens, fathers reading the paper in the living rooms, children playing in the fenced yards. There were real cars in the garages. They put up schools, water towers, barns, and sheds; they penned in flocks of living sheep, chickens, and cattle.

The army, for its part, dressed department-store dummies in military uniforms and propped them up in the open. They set up mothballed artillery pieces, tanks, airplanes, whole fake military encampments. They even dressed Chester White pigs in specially tailored fatigue uniforms to test the thermal capacity of army-issue clothing.

Then the AEC blasted the whole thing to pulp and pieces—pigs, cows, sheep, equipment, dummies, little towns, schools, water towers, all smashed and shivered. Later, when the Geiger counters cooled down a bit, the AEC took the news media in to view the destruction. They bunkered cameras in strategic places and took film footage that was later released to the public, showing in slow motion the houses suddenly being torched, then flying apart, lumber and plumbing ripped out and flung aside, exposing the gaping foundations; mannequins suddenly melting, torn up and hurled away by the astonishing heat and force.

"Turk" was a heavy-yield shot, and most of the troops in camp were sent out to witness it. Awakened at 3:00 A.M., we assembled around a line of khaki buses, wearing fatigue jackets with liners, combat boots, helmet pots. The ride to the forward area was long, but there was no talking or singing. Some of the men went back to sleep; most stared out at the darkness.

When we stepped off the troop buses, the desert sky was cold, immense, and shimmering. We stood shivering in ranks on the sand while officers swaggered in front of us. We were told the explosion was scheduled for an hour hence, and then procedures were reviewed again. We were to follow orders exactly and to be extremely cautious. Ranks broke, troops moved out into the desert and began filing into the trenches, and I went off to find Womble.

Some men were joking nervously, teasing each other about whether they should say their prayers or bid each other good-bye. One guy asked his buddy if he thought he could light a cigarette by sticking the tip of it over the trench top. "You'd probably burn your fucking nose off," his buddy said. Mostly we felt helpless and were quiet.

"Thirty minutes to ground zero," a voice grated from a loudspeaker behind the trench lines, as if announcing a bus schedule. Standing in the trenches, we were given permission to smoke.

Womble lit up beside me. I could tell he didn't feel like talking. I was just glad to be with him. We stood together for ten minutes in silence, watching early light stroke across the horizon.

Then the wind shifted above the aurora. I remember wondering aloud to Womble whether it would make a difference to the drift of radiation. I was hoping this might cause them to call the whole thing off. Womble said, "It ain't in our hands."

As the count grew short, we were given the order to crouch, and tension grew palpable. Sergeant Easter, Womble's platoon sergeant, began a monologue. Easter had been raised on a hog farm in Missouri. He was a heavy man with a gentle touch who spoke rarely and always weighed his words. His orders were

succinct, direct, but he often gave the men homilies from his
rural background to instruct them.

Some magpies fussed in brittlebush, and the air was chill
and dry across the blasted desert flats. Easter's words seemed
such pathetic things and at first appeared to make no sense at
all. Yet I knew him well enough to realize that, in his country
way of parables, he was attempting to put some name to or
give some explanation for this unspeakable thing we were
ordered to do. He was trying to do his job and give his men
courage, attempting to take the edge off our fear with a story.
But wedged in and bent over as he was in those dismal
trenches, his shaking Missouri twang was strained.

As we sweated and breathed hard, not trying to disguise
our fear anymore, he told us about "blood lock." He talked
lightly through his nose, his voice high, telling us how his
father and he and his brothers kept fifty pigs on their farm in
Missouri. When slaughter time came, they would run them
into the yard, where he and his brother chased them down and
dragged them one at a time to their father, who pulled a knife
across their throats.

I don't know why he chose to talk about his pigs out there
on an atomic battlefield. Perhaps because they called us guinea
pigs—or because he had been disturbed by the animals
burned and blown apart in the previous test shots. He was
frightened and releasing tension. I can't remember his exact
words, but Easter ended his story with this extraordinary
caveat:

"Pig can scream even when its pipe's slit. Falls down in its
own blood and rolls like it's tryin' to get it back inside its skin.
There'd be half a dozen still twitchin' around before we'd cinch
'em up on the frame to bleed. Then my ol' man'd make us stop
for a while. We'd go down in the barn and drink well water, sit
together for a spell in the cool. Blood lock, the old man'd warn

us. You boys best remember this. It can turn your soul to red. It's a thing that, if it ever gets ahold of you, makes you want to go on killin' till you drop."

There was silence for a moment when the parable was finished. Then a tense, anonymous voice said, "Shut the fuck up, Easter!" There were no more words after this, except those from the loudspeaker. "Three minutes to ground zero."

We hunkered down in those coarse, crumbling trenches and tucked our heads in, putting our hands over our eyes. Birds began their small songs at traces of dawn. Someone farted loudly, but no one laughed or complained. "Two minutes to ground zero," the guy on the loudspeaker rasped, cutting away our time, cutting away our breath.

Normally we count sequentially from zero to higher numbers. Even when a boxer is down the count is linear. We count our pulses progressively, and our money and our years. But when things are tense and staged, when we're not sure what is going to happen, we tend to count backward down to a point where nothing is left. Is it a sign of latent regret?

I can tell you *I* was regretting. And we were out there in front, in those sepulchral slit trenches, testing someone else's anxiety. Men were making small, wavering, high-pitched sounds. "One minute to ground zero," the voice said. "Thirty seconds to ground zero." Then, "Ten-nine-eight-seven-six-five-four-three-two-one-zero."

The flash was a sudden, immense snap of heat, an all-pervasive burst of light that enveloped us, got under our helmets, into our shoes, over our backs, through our navels into our stomachs. I could see my finger bones x-rayed as I held them over my eyes.

There was a slight shifting and sighing in the trenches. Then within seconds we heard and felt the shock wave thundering toward us like a stampede. It didn't just sweep in, but crushed onto us with enormous power. The earth and air exploded, then we were suffocating and there was no air, only heavy blackness. We were weighed down under rocks and sand—the trench side had caved in, burying us. We were a row of live corpses, howling, cursing, crawling over each other, clawing ourselves out of our graves. The earth was in our ears and eyes and mouths, weighing our legs down, bearing down our arms.

No one had warned us of this. As I think back now, only Dante can serve such a scene. In *The Inferno,* Virgil has led Dante to the fiery Pit of Hell. The infinite groans are like thunder. Virgil says to Dante that he will lead him into the blind world below, and Virgil, already terrified, cries out his hesitation to be led by someone who already seems pallid with fear.

The first men out began pulling the others, sputtering and pouring off grit and pebbles. Someone gave me a hand and yanked me up from the dirt. My eyes full of sand, ears ringing like air-raid sirens, I could dimly hear officers shouting. No one paid attention to them. The earth was immediate, threatening, suffocating. In such conditions, the only authority is survival.

We dusted ourselves and each other off, emptied the dirt from our steel pots, blew our noses, wiped our eyes. Womble was out, standing beside me, but when I reached to brush off his field jacket, I realized that something was very wrong. It was like touching a machine running hard. He had done nothing to clean himself off and was vibrating with shock. The specter of death, the feeling of live burial, must have broken something in him. I could see, in the light from the explosion, that his face was covered with gray dust and his eyes were not focusing. I grabbed him by his shoulders and shook him hard.

"Jesus Christ!" someone called out.

I looked up. An immense fireball boiled and sucked in on itself as it drove up, erupting, blazing infernally, glowing in multiple colors, topping high with ice. It seemed to reach out over our heads. As its fires began to cool, it pulsated and rumbled, turning a malevolent purple in the dawn light, seeming to tilt slightly toward us on its stalk in the morning crosswinds. I looked at the men around me—aghast, humbled, arms hanging, mouths open.

Letting go of Womble, I stood with the others, craning our necks, numbed, as if we were witnessing some evil anti-god assaulting heaven. Ahead I could see radiological safety jeeps backing out of their dugouts, headlights glowing through the dust as they started their drive toward the fire with Geiger counters. The officers were shouting again. We were to move forward, follow the rad-safe teams.

Men began shuffling along. I looked at Womble. His tongue was hanging out; his eyes remained unfocused. I brushed more dust off, gave him another shake. "Come on, baby. We've got to go forward now."

Womble had locked his knees. He wasn't going anywhere. A second lieutenant came up, a little ROTC guy. He barked at us, circling like a terrier.

"I think he's in shock, sir," I told the lieutenant. "We got buried over here."

"Get him moving!" the little guy yapped. "These troops are going forward." He gave Womble a push.

"Hey, don't touch him, sir," I said. "Hands off. I'll get him moving."

He looked at my name tag. Even out there, under the fire of hell on earth, he considered making me lock my heels and stand at attention for insubordination. Thank God he moved on.

I grasped Womble's head and turned his face toward me. "Womble! No shit, man. We've got to walk. Come on, big guy." He focused, and I held his elbow for a moment. He took a step and we were moving together, two guys from Ohio, witnessing the blind world, walking toward the center of Hades.

Womble was never the same after Turk. The burial experience took a large chunk of his psyche, and he lost more ground with each subsequent test. Sergeant Easter noticed this and talked to him about reassignment, but Womble wouldn't even take sick call, wanted to face his devils down and stick it out. When we got together he was feckless and preoccupied. Nothing renewed his spirit—no baseball or jazz talk, no women, nothing. He wouldn't discuss his plans for the future anymore, even though he was getting close to being discharged.

I hadn't seen him for a while when I heard that he'd had trouble with the Las Vegas police. Apparently he had gone into town with some friends, gotten bored with the casinos, left his buddies to take a walk, and wandered into a residential area. It was night and the police stopped him. I guess he gave them some back talk, so they made him lean up against the cruiser and walloped his ribs a few times with a blackjack. As they were pulling away they saw he was taking down the number of their cruiser, so they backed up, got out, and pounded him some more. Womble complained to his company commander and the military police, and they promised to check with the Vegas police, but nothing happened.

The test series ended and we were shutting down Camp Desert Rock for the year. I was packing crates in the public information office one morning when the head clerk came in and said, "Zimmer, you better go see Womble. He's supposed to be shipping out for discharge, but he's juiced out of his mind. Nobody can do anything with him. Sergeant Easter asked me to come get you. Maybe you can talk to him. His CO says he's going to take his stripe and hold him in quarters if he doesn't straighten out."

I found him alone, wavering round on his company street, scatting quietly to himself. No one else was in sight. His broad, strong back was turned away from me. I went up and gave him a bump on his shoulder.

When he turned around his mustache was twitching. He was expecting trouble, his right hand cocked, ready to punch someone hard. I backpedaled until he recognized me.

"Hey, Dad!" he said, giving me his smile and relaxing.

"Womble, what are you doing?"

"Having a little taste, man."

"Kind of early in the morning?"

"Not too bad, Dad. Makes things better."

"Let's go get some coffee."

"Not today, Dad. No coffee, no time. Got to get my papers and go."

"Well, let's move around a little. I need to talk to you before you go."

So we walked together again, Solomon Womble and I. Hades had cooled down, but we needed to keep moving.

"Gonna re-up, Dad," he said.

"Don't tell me that, Womble! What is this? What about the psychology?"

"Ain't no psychology," he said. "No psychology. You dig?"

"But re-up, man? Get straight. What's that going to do for you?"

"Army's got shovels. I need a shovel."

We walked for a long time out into the sand and back, not worrying about snakes or scorpions or any other indigenous creatures of the desert, and he started to come around. But there was no persuading him. He was going to go back to Cleveland for a few weeks, drink all the booze in town and screw all the women, blow his severance pay, then reenlist. I knew he would walk away from me if I kept pushing it. He didn't want to discuss the future anymore. We talked a little about Larry Doby and Coleman Hawkins and Charlie Parker. We went into his mess hall and he ate noon chow. He was still shaky, but making it now. I went with him to his company office while he picked up his papers. Sergeant Easter said good-bye and shook his hand. Womble's CO came out of his office for a moment, glared, but didn't say anything—not even good-bye.

Three years after this, the army closed down Camp Desert Rock for good, leveled the shacks and Quonset huts, hauled the equipment away, and bulldozed the foundations, burying the concrete rubble, boards, old pipes, and corrugated steel in the sand. The United States government has not tested atomic bombs in the open since 1963.

But on that day in 1955, Womble and I exchanged addresses, promised to write, stay in touch, maybe get together for a Cleveland Indians game sometime. I went with him to the bus stand and waited until the Las Vegas coach drove up.

"Catch you later, Dad," he said. We shook hands and he got on. I stood under the overhang as the bus idled. Womble sat looking straight ahead until it began moving, then he gave me a last quick look from his window. Forty-five years have gone by. I think of him with these words.

Trouble

Even now, all these years later, I sometimes awaken from bad dreams tasting the grit of the desert. My ears have never stopped ringing. Witnessing atomic bombs was the trouble of my young manhood; now, decades later, ill winds were blowing again.

We bought the farm joyfully and for ten years traveled back and forth from Iowa City on weekends. It was our great blessing—and my curse. We arrived at the beginnings of weekends, always in happy anticipation, and I reveled in the hours for poetry, reading, walking, doing chores, but as the time drew close for our departure, my spirits inevitably declined. I tried hard, but there was no escaping my feelings of frustration. For the first time in my life I began to resent work because it interfered with poetry. It was a difficult period in the book business, and this did not help my mood.

I first became a "boss" when I was twenty-seven and placed in charge of some book warehousing operations. From then on I always had people assigned to work under my direction. I took the responsibility seriously; over the years I managed carefully and rarely had problems with staff or management. But now there were troubles: budgetary restraints, maligning by colleagues and friends, the posturing of superiors. I became

impatient with academic and administrative windbags, and
some lazy, perfidious coworkers. I became a salty fellow with
paranoid feelings—a king-sized pain in the ass myself.
Although four books of my poems were published while I was
at Iowa, I was perceived only as a sixty-three-year-old man in
charge of an office employing six women. The whispering
began.

As the staff grew colder to me, I began to admit to myself
some of my misgivings about them: my distaste for their social
attitudes; their sometimes undisciplined, relentlessly cause-
oriented feminism that gave little credence to tradition and
verities, and no credit to anything "man" had ever done.

The word was that I had lost more than a step in aging,
agonized too audibly about the troubled state of the book
business. I still had old-fashioned notions about leadership—
but decades as a "boss" had not taught me how to cope with
this situation. I was no longer useful or tolerable. My choice
was to spend two years fighting for control and coping with
treacherous, petulant people, or resign and retire early to the
driftless hills.

I had worked as a scholarly publisher for three decades. When
I first began attending the national conventions of the associa-
tion of university presses, I was in awe of the elders who were
officers and chief participants in this organization. These venerable directors moved with an assurance and bravura that I
admired and coveted as a young man.

But over the years, as I watched the changes in their ranks,
I began to observe what often seemed to be troubled, difficult
passages as the elders grew close to retirement. These emi-
nences were not infrequently challenged, and they became
worn and worried as the years mounted. Even the most articulate and artful began at some point to falter. Apparently,
directing a university press was an enervating and hazardous

business. Rumors abounded that these people were failing, had misjudged, mismanaged, fallen behind in unacceptable ways, or otherwise lost control. Their colleagues, their editorial boards, and inevitably their administrators were putting heat on them and had them under duress.

When I was in my apprentice years as a scholarly publisher, being the wag that I was, I developed a theory of geezerhood. At the national conventions I joked with my younger colleagues about the process of geezerhood, sometimes making book with them on when the first signs of faltering and erosion would occur among our elders. There were ultimate geezers, medium geezers, and minor geezers, but few completely escaped the frazzling visitation of geezerhood. I noted that the larger percentage of older directors moved on—or were moved on—to their golden years under heavy fire or at least thick clouds of gloom and rumor. There was an illusion of happy gratification, but it did not seem authentic.

When they were gone—they were gone. Their presses and the organization of university presses continued unabated without them. Their legends disappeared almost instantly into the ether and they were abandoned as Lewis and Clark claimed some Indian tribes discarded their "poor, old superannuated wretches" along the trail.

And so in time it was with me—and there were not even any illusions of happy gratification. The gods punished me for my wiseacre theorizing. I had become a super geezer. A woman recently told me she was surprised by my story, at the depth of my misunderstanding. She likened me to other men in their sixties she had met who seemed thus out of touch, bewildered by feminism, annoyingly unaware that their chivalrous and paternalistic words and actions are too often received as condescending and patronizing.

Okay. Okay. I had developed bad habits over forty years. I had thrown my gears into cruise and was oblivious to the sig-

nals, maintaining a kind of restrained benevolence that was
now resented. What had served me well enough before was
now hopelessly out of date. As Lear ranted in Act V: "Pray you,
undo this button." I was blowing it big time.

I had made the mistake of faltering and growing older, I
worried about the disturbing state of the book business, I
wanted to be a poet—and I was a man. Shame on me!
Thoreau writes, "But men labor under a mistake. The better
part of the man is soon plowed into the soil for compost. By
a seeming fate, commonly called necessity, they are employed,
as it says in an old book, laying up treasures which moth and
rust will corrupt and thieves break through and steal. It is a
fool's life, as they will find when they get to the end of it, if
not before."

I met with my colleagues and spoke in anger about their back-
biting. They moved to the edge of their chairs, did not feel they
had to listen to me, had told tales to my superiors and finessed
my authority, felt no obligation to hear my comments—these
people, all of whom I had hired, encouraged, promoted, and
given *my* raises to. As their final gesture, they stood up and
walked out, leaving me with my desolation.

> No, I'll not weep;
> I have full cause for weeping, but this heart
> Shall break into a hundred, thousand flaws
> Or ere I'll weep. O fool! I shall go mad.

But I had no fool. I sat alone in my office among pictures,
dictionaries, keepsakes, pens, papers, typewriter, manuscripts,
computer, in box, out box—the residue of half a century of
work. My phone rang and rang. For a while I ignored it, but
the habit of duty is not lost in a day. I gathered my strength to
pick up the receiver. It was my boss. Apparently he had been
cued by one of my staff. He asked how I was doing.

How did he know I was *doing* anything? I told him I was destroyed. He assured me that I still had much to look forward to. Then—as God is my witness—in the midst of my desolation, as profound feelings of loss and betrayal were overwhelming my spirit, he said he knew I was distressed and wanted to make certain I was not planning to do something violent, like bomb the university press.

My God! It was time to go. Road-weary, vulnerable, and diminished after forty years, I retired under my own cloud of gloom and rumor, without any sense of reward for my years of hard work. Instead of celebration at the end of my forty years in the book business, I was endowed with memories of graceless perfidy, cowardice, and ingratitude. Few days pass when I do not, at some point, still feel this pain. All the work, the hours, years, pleasures, teamwork, devotion to duties, triumphs, and failures were suddenly cast in shadow. The books I had seen into print over three decades—more than a thousand—seemed like victims on a killing ground. The years and years of buying and selling manuscripts, contracts, late-night shuffling of typewritten pages, phone calls, inventory runs, negotiations, planning, correspondence, requisitions, budgets, trips, decisions, all were wreckage washed up on a storm beach.

I began retirement in shock, reeling with monstrous misgivings. But I kept my eye on the ball and started doing what I had always wanted to do—write to my heart's content every day for as long as I wished. Despite my anguish over the subterfuge and ugliness of my last days of work, I began to realize that I had been blessed now to indulge my gift. In fact, it was glorious license, a lifelong dream come true. I proceeded deliberately and did not push, and the words eased my pain, led me to nooks and crannies in my psyche that had been unexplored for years.

Gradually I began to regain my pride.

Dogs

IF YOU PAY ATTENTION TO DOGS, they can help you
through the very worst patches of your life. I have counted
heavily on them. Being with them is an important part of my
life. Wanda was the first dog that came to the driftless hills
with us. She was magnificent, mostly Great Dane, big and
stately. She loved walks in the fields and woods, and she barked
at us incessantly until we took her out, but she stayed close and
did not romp off into the brush like our other dogs had. She
charged after deer and chased them across fields until they
reached the trees, but then she would stop and return to us for
praise. When
she was really moving across the grass she rippled like a horse.
She weighed over a hundred and thirty pounds, with a massive chest. Alas, she was doomed by her largeness. She died
suddenly, not quite six years of age. Sometimes big dogs do
not live long lives. The veterinarian could not explain her
death and we declined an autopsy. She was gone and we were
desolate.

That dog could sing! She puckered her lips into an O,
beginning with small swallowing sounds, then rising to power
and resonance, gulping air to continue with passion and a
flawless sense of canine musical form. Her voice was high and

beautiful. I sang with her and we joined in many fine songs: "Body and Soul," "Naima," "The Trout," "Jeg elsker Dig," "My Rosary," "Perdido," and dozens of others. Our production number was "Stardust."

She loved the farm. When we drove in on weekends and passed through the fence marking our property she would sing and moan, so happy she could barely contain herself. We had to let her out at the first curve in the dirt road, and she galloped enthusiastically after the truck the rest of the way in.

When the corn was high I gave her ripe ears to carry in her mouth like bones. The yellow bones. She dug great holes and buried them, then forgot where she had placed them. I made up yellow-bone poems for her and chanted them. "I will arise and go now / and go to the yellow bone . . ." "As I was young and easy under the yellow bone . . ." "The yellow bone that rubs its back against the window pane . . ."

She cut her leg on some barbed wire while I was off on a trip. Suzanne took her to the veterinarian, and when I arrived home Wanda was lying miserably under a blanket on the couch. Suzanne explained in solicitous tones what had happened. When I approached Wanda to commiserate with her, she reached her wounded leg out from under the blanket for me to inspect.

She loved to carry sticks, too, and drove me daffy when I was breaking up branches for kindling. She couldn't understand why I was smashing up all this good stuff, these wonderful toys, so she dragged them back into the fields to protect them.

But then she got sick and there was no cure. She kept collapsing. We got her up and walked her around, but her long, powerful legs could not support her, and she fell again. Dogs do not like to fall down; it demoralizes them, is the very worst thing that can happen to them. We tried different veterinarians, and finally had her admitted to the veterinary clinic in

Gays Mills where they put her on an IV and ran tests. Suzanne
went in to register her and I sat with her in the bed of the
pickup. Her eyes were open and she breathed slowly. I pressed
my forehead against hers and tried to start a song, "Only a
Rose," "St. James Infirmary." But her spirit was withdrawing
and she was far away. The next day the doctor called to say she
had died. We were disconsolate, alternately holding each other
and weeping. For months after, we saw her sweet black form
wandering in the fields and stretched out in her favorite places
in the house.

The best thing we did was to find a new dog almost immediately. We did not wish to replace the irreplaceable Wanda; we
wanted a dog as different from her as possible. From the local
pound we got a bearded collie named Bathsheba. We have no
idea where she came from. Someone had cut off her tail when
she was a whelp. She was small, obviously the runt of the litter.
A university student had found her wandering in Iowa City
near Interstate 80 and took care of her until classes were over,
then turned her in to the Animal Rescue League. She is black
and white with brown eyes and a capacious nose. She weighs
about thirty-five pounds and her hair is long and shaggy until
we have it trimmed for summer. In cold weather it puffs up
like electric shock. She has freckles inside her mouth and on
her snout where the hair is worn off from her rooting.

She was about four months old when she came to our
house. We took her for walks in the country and she struggled
in the tall field grass, so I tucked her under my arm and carried
her like a loaf of warm bread.

Now she has been with us for eight years. She is not a
singer, but she is a most discerning listener. Every afternoon,
before we take a nap together, I sing her name in love songs
and artistic chants, and she requires skill and spirit in my
falsetto voice. If I sing well and with true feeling, she is very

moved and turns to place a paw across her snout and closes her eyes, sighing like a girl I held and danced with years ago.

She has the powerful rear legs of a herding dog and is a great darter and sprinter, able to run down small animals. Her first kill was a squirrel; I think she surprised herself. Eventually she ate it, but first she rolled on the corpse, hauled it around in triumph, and would not let us near it. She was very proud of herself.

She caught a young rabbit in the woods and, rather than abandon it as carrion, she ate the whole thing. For a while she strutted like a young lion. Later, we were having a drink on the deck when I noticed she was looking glassy-eyed. Suddenly she regurgitated the whole glutinous bunny at our feet, in the reverse order of how she had eaten it, head coming out last.

She is also—I must say it—a bit of a ghoul, enjoying particularly wretched bits of gopher and squirrel jerky sunk in the fields or left on the gravel road by the hawks and coyotes. She delights in rolling in unmitigated pooh, is very selective in picking what must surely be the corpses of leprous skunks to luxuriate in. When she appears at the door with her long hair thus perfumed and decorated, she cannot understand why we shout and march her immediately to the garden hose.

Once she ate a whole nest of baby horned larks. Suzanne was furious with her. The other day she found a deer leg bone and trotted around gripping it in her mouth like a baton. When she sees a group of deer munching on the inclines of the fields she approaches partway and barks at them. The deer have grown used to her and now are unmoved. They hold and gaze at her as they masticate. This is a terrible frustration for Sheba, a kind of indignity she does not suffer willingly. She advances a bit closer and barks more stridently until they start. Then and only then, when she is certain they are in full retreat, will she charge after them and chase them to the edge of the woods.

Some of these tales might sound like complaints, but this is hardly the case. Sheba is a large portion of our contentment, a diversion we adore. We are a happy trinity up in the driftless hills, harmony just like the Mills Brothers, amused and delighting in each other's company. We depend on each other. I was despairing one day about my work problems, my eyes clenched tight as I paced, and suddenly felt soft, small paws on my thighs. Sheba had come to me and was standing on her hinders to comfort me. I count on her for a great deal, and just being near her helped me in my troubles.

We find big furry scats on our gravel road and strange prints in the mud, shaped like four horned moons over a mountain. Sheba noses these things and tenses her ears, spreads her nostrils, squats, and signs her presence. On occasion at night she wakes us from deep slumber with a harsh bark, blending into a tremolo howl—three times she does this by the open window, joining the distant call and chorus of coyotes. Next morning when we walk she watches the foggy woods, as if recollecting some older life. Days like this we become uneasy, grow overloving and insecure, fearing she might consider abandoning us. But she favors us with constancy. Perhaps it is custom or fear that holds her. We choose to imagine it is love.

Old Jazz

I ALWAYS THOUGHT OF RETIREMENT as a warm good-bye, a memorable sayonara, a happy finish to anticipate, but conditions did not permit me this reward. Despair overwhelmed my last weeks and months of work; frustration and anger filled my hours and days.

My instincts were good. I needed greatness—contact with human and powerful art—to help me endure the invidiousness and humiliation. I went back to basic texts, reread *King Lear, Pere Goriot, Beowulf, Return of the Native, Walden, The Tower*. I looked at Brueghel's peasants, Manet's last flowers, Cézanne's fruit, Pissarro's landscapes, Steichen's and Kuhn's photographs. I listened to Bach's cello suites, Handel's operas, Beethoven's quartets, any Mozart, Mahler's and Schubert's great songs.

But nothing offered more comfort than jazz. Here was a great irony: I had a tape player in my office, but even with my office door shut and solo piano playing at low volume, my colleagues complained that jazz disturbed them. Lord! Of course it did. I wasn't doing anything right, and was even creating further scandal by taunting them with Bud Powell. So my days were artless, but my nights and weekends were full of great jazz.

Why do I love this music? Because it articulates happiness. It states pain and loss. It is ordinary, yet elegant. It tells us how to die and how to stay alive. It heals us and nurtures our spirit. It evokes youth, tells of love perfect and imperfect. It reminds us that we are human and vulnerable. It keeps time as it suspends time. The time you spend listening to jazz—like the time Thoreau spent standing in silence—is a bonus. If you listen well, you will never grow old, despite what the body does.

Again I went for basic texts: Lester Young, Duke Ellington, Coleman Hawkins, John Coltrane, Ben Webster, Art Tatum, Thelonious Monk, Charlie Parker. Their strength and inventiveness have sustained me through difficult times—through the experience of atomic bombs and appalling faithlessness.

As always, Count Basie provided the groundwork. Ever since I first heard those great roaring, measured sounds half a century ago, his music has been part of my life. But now, instead of tickling my young libido and titillating me with promises of adulthood, it rolls out memories—large, happy, comforting reminders that there is life beyond toil and trouble. Breakneck or sensuous, the music is wise and imperfectly perfect. It is Basie out in front, with his piano, the antithesis of his big stomping band, leading in, punctuating lightly, and giving direction. Thank God for him—he's been going down all my life, swinging merrily or moaning low, carrying me through my best and worst hours.

Young Jazz

*Keep your eyes on the fellow at the piano. The sparrow. He don't
know nothing, but just keep your eyes on him and we'll all be
together on what's going down.*

Count Basie

FAT CARLSON AND I used to go to the movies on winter
Saturday afternoons in 1945. We would meet at the bus stop
and ride downtown to the Palace Theatre on Market Street in
Canton, Ohio. One weekend the marquee announced that our
Abbott and Costello movie was paired with a live matinee performance of the Count Basie Orchestra. Uncertain about what
this meant, we decided to forgo our milk shakes to make up
the difference in ticket price. Both of us were eleven years old.
I cannot speak for Fat, but it was a sacrifice that significantly
changed my life.

After Abbott and Costello's knockabout, the theater stayed
dark. There was a pause, a rustling and scraping of chairs,
then a piano started jiving, and someone on a loudspeaker
announced the Basie band. The screen lifted slowly and the
band was revealed, bathed in blue light, saxophones swinging
the riffs of Basie's theme, "One O'Clock Jump." The trumpets

and trombones roared into the tune together, then the trumpets jumped out and hit it hard over the driving saxophones. I was transported, bouncing in my seat, surprised, overwhelmed by sensuous rhythm and sound.

They alternated jump tunes and dance numbers, and I could barely contain myself. There were acts. A tap dancer named Peg Leg Bates came out and stomped around on one leg and a wooden limb, worrying us that he might fall, but he was amazingly deft. A beautiful black woman sang the blues.

Count Basie was out in front on the piano, smiling his complete smile, moving the band, driving it in and out of numbers through the big, powerful solos and roaring section work. Midway through the show he brought out a line of chorus girls, and they pranced and bumped into each other gorgeously on the stage. I could smell their perfume up in the balcony. The band closed out with an easy "Rock-a-Bye Basie," then roared back into a chorus of "One O'Clock Jump."

When it was over I was tingling. I beat my little hands together until they were pink. I tried to talk Fat into staying for another show, but he said his mom was expecting him home. He seemed a little stunned, but all the way home on the bus I gabbed about the music.

I think I was born to love jazz. I tuned in as a small child, when my parents allowed me to stay up late on Wednesday nights, to listen to Bing Crosby's radio show. Usually he had show business guest stars like Dinah Shore or Bob Hope, but one evening he featured Louis Armstrong and some musicians. Satchmo and Bing crooned and bantered, but I got most excited when the musicians—Baby Dodds, Joe Venuti, Trummy Young, and the incredible Louis—started cooking by themselves. I had never heard anything so swift and engaging. I was a sickly kid and had been down for a week with the croup, but I hopped around in my sleepers in front of our big Philco like a spring bunny. My

parents were impressed and probably a little alarmed, because
I had never been so animated before. The next morning I still
had jazz in my head, and my lungs were clear. I got up volun-
tarily, put on my clothes, and went back to school.

On Sunday afternoons there was a network radio show
called *Piano Playhouse,* and my father tuned in as we ate dinner.
Usually the pianists were slick, popular players like Alec Temple-
ton, Carmen Cavallero, and Frankie Carle, but sometimes it
was Meade Lux Lewis, Teddy Wilson, or Art Tatum—and that
put some snap into the roast chicken and mashed potatoes.
Even then I could hear and feel the difference. The iced tea
would be jumping in the glasses until my father ordered me to
stop kicking the table leg.

A few years later when my future brother-in-law, Bob, was
courting my sister, he would visit us in Ohio during summer
vacations from college. One time he brought a Duke Ellington
album. I could not stop listening. I loved the flag-wavers like
"Jam with Sam" and "Take the A Train" but also grooved on
more mellow pieces like "Mood Indigo" and "In a Sentimental
Mood." We had a console record cabinet in the living room, so
I was right in the middle of things. Over and over I would put
those platters on. My family had to push me out the door to
play baseball with my friends, but as soon as I came back I
would set the needle down on the vinyl again. I could not get
enough. In those days there were no earphones, so everyone in
the house had to listen. Finally they persuaded me to turn the
volume way down and press my ear to the speaker.

I had heard big, ricky-ticky bands like those of Sammy
Kaye, Guy Lombardo, and Kay Kaiser on the radio, and I had
heard Basie's big, swinging band at the Palace, but never anything with the élan of the Ellington orchestra. Of course,
Johnny Hodges knocked me out, but all the great soloists
swept me up with their art and sophistication. The ensemble
work was a thrill—those marvelous tones coming together,

creating a full, lush, sexy sound on slow-tempo songs, and
when the band cooked on the upbeat tunes, I soared with it.
I could not keep my feet still or my shoulders from bobbing.
The album notes told how Ellington and the band traveled the
world. Parisians loved their savoir faire. The great music halls
of London were SRO. This seemed so remote and exotic to me
as I headed into puberty in the middle of Ohio.

Realizing how much I enjoyed the Ellington album, Bob
"accidentally" left it on the console. He almost lost favor with
my parents, but it was an act of great generosity. The next
time he came to visit, he helped me solder a jack to the white
Motorola tabletop in my room, and we wired it so I could plug
in a turntable and listen to jazz records through my radio
without driving everyone nuts.

What was it about this music that swept me up so completely? Why is it still so important to me? My cherished
recollections are as rich as the times of actual listening. I can
be miles from a stereo, but memories and echoes help me get
through a long day.

Some people cannot hear jazz. I once spent a bundle taking
a girl I very much admired to one of the jazz variety shows
that traveled city auditoriums in the 1950s and 1960s. It was to
be our big night—Ellington, Erroll Garner, Sarah Vaughan,
Stan Getz. I was vibrating, but she sat on her hands all night,
looking bored or threatened. I did not take her out afterward
for a snack. I took her home, opened her door, eased her in, and
said goodnight. No kisses. No need to waste any more time.

A good friend once asked me why I liked this "cacophony."
I gave him another chance, telling him to calm down and listen
again. He pretended to put his ear to it but could not wait to
ask the question again. I have not seen him for years.

So jazz is important enough to end a love or a friendship,
and generous enough to cure a sick little kid. What else does it
do? I found out early.

There was another girl I liked a lot when I was in high school. One summer evening I walked to her house and saw her through the window in a clinch with one of my friends. I almost collapsed on the lawn. I staggered home in agony, my heart crushed to pulp. I went to my room, lay down on the bed, and wept. The pain would not go away; I had to do something.

I had been buying "Jazz at the Philharmonic" albums with money I scratched up from my paper route. I put on Volume 13, "Embraceable You"—Roy Eldridge, Lester Young, Charlie Parker, Tommy Turk, Flip Phillips, Hank Jones, Buddy Rich, Ray Brown. After a Jones introduction, Eldridge opens with a warm, pristine solo. Then Lester Young comes in with just a short solo, exactly two minutes, followed by Parker, Turk, Parker again, and then Phillips closing, all playing gorgeously and with feeling. But it was Lester Young's solo that got me through that night of pain so long ago. "Embraceable You" is hardly the blues, but Pres was playing something that nudged my sky-blue funk. I listened and listened again, literally wearing a groove into his part of the platter. I had always been fascinated by his solo, sensing its wisdom and accomplishment, but I had not fully understood it. He put his gentle eroticism and sadness right out in front. Phrase after phrase— no secrets, only pure feeling changing and building the tune. That night I understood perfectly.

Two minutes *exactly*. With embouchure, warm breath, spittle, a long, graceful curve of brass tubing, magnificent talent, and great heart, Lester Young, a southern black man who had lived a life I could not even imagine—threatened and cheated by racism all his life—was stating my pain and comforting me, a brokenhearted white teenager in the middle of Ohio.

That tender, long-distance connection is what makes jazz significant and endearing. When I am in the dumps, I still run that memorized solo through my head. Its meaning has changed for me, but it remains part of my life. So Pres connects even now with a retired sixty-six-year-old geezer living atop a hill in southwest Wisconsin, half a century after he played his solo at Carnegie Hall. This is enduring art with its ability to quicken, sadden, and yet sustain.

Finding jazz in a smaller Midwestern city in the late 1940s and the 1950s took some effort. The downtown news depot in Canton stocked *Downbeat* for local musicians, and I bought copies when I could afford them. Most of my first records were swing music, but I became fascinated with bebop. When I could not find records in local shops, I special-ordered them from the New York wholesalers who advertised in *Downbeat*. I became a curiosity at the post office. The packages would not fit into our mailbox, so the mailman would leave a pick-up slip. I had to ask my father to run me downtown to the post office after work, and he would hassle me loudly all the way to the delivery window about how I was wasting my money. Then the postal clerk would bring me a package from New York City marked Bebop Incorporated or How High the Moon Records and hand it to me with a curious look. My father was incredulous.

I did not always know what I was buying. There were no jazz radio shows, so I ordered blind—records by musicians I had read about in *Downbeat*. Usually, to be certain, I went for titles that had a "bop" pun in them: "As I Live and Bop," "Bop, Look, and Listen," "Boptimism," "Boplicity," "Cubano Bop," "Bop Sign." I could only afford so much, but I bought quite a range, from Brew Moore to Bird, Dodo Marmarosa to Thelonious Monk. I loved every one of those slick black platters that whirled like turbines on my 78 rpm spindle. They came from faraway smoky cities of intrigue and elegant corruption, and the guys who made them were the coolest people I could imagine. When I cracked a disk it caused me great pain. I would press it flat on the turntable and play it anyway, putting up with the *pop, pop, pop* to hear the music. Sometimes only a little half-moon chip would break off, but at least I had the larger part of the tune.

I invited my buddies up to my room to listen, and we bounced around from wall to wall, giggling and happy. "Where are you getting these hot records?" they asked. One time I broke my bed, jumping on it to show off, fracturing the wooden legs. "Some chips just flew," Steve Endres said. The dancing stopped and my dad shut down my record buying for a while.

My pal Dick Schiavone's older brother was an alto saxophonist who gigged around town when he was not going to college. Dick had a job as a caddy at a golf course and made enough money to buy his own duds. He would have his pants pegged and wore pink shirts with Mr. B roll collars like his brother.

I got into a tremendous row with my mother in a clothing store when I told her I wanted to have the cuffs pegged on the new brown pants we had selected.

"Absolutely not."

"How about just a little?"

"No."

I could not persuade her that she was being unreasonable. I needed at least a token. No one would notice if there was just a *slight* tuck.

"No."

"But it is the style!"

"It is *not* the style."

I could not tell her it was the way jazz musicians dressed. That would have made things worse. My mother was the daughter of an immigrant French miner and a Belgian waitress. Only gangsters and low people wore their pants pegged.

But I was tired of going around looking like Dopey Danny Dee.

She insisted I must look neat and presentable.

Hell. Somewhere—I cannot remember where—I found an old pair of discarded chartreuse flannel trousers that were a little long on my legs and large around my waist. I took them with some of my paper route money to the tailor shop around the corner from my father's shoe store. The Jewish tailor looked at me over the top of his glasses when I told him I wanted them taken in at the waist, shortened . . . and pegged. He knew my father, of course.

"You are certain?"

Yes, I was certain.

I wore them once with a bright yellow shirt. It was not right. I did not look cool like Schiavone or Lester Young. I looked like a stalk of pale asparagus in bloom. Eventually the pants disappeared from my closet. I suspect my mother confiscated them. I beat the game anyway by tucking the legs of my blue jeans at the bottom and rolling them up to look pegged. My parents would not let me get my hair duck-tailed either, but I still knew more about jazz than anyone in the neighborhood. I affected a kind of jazz musician shuffle. Lefty Rowles called me "Jazzy Zimbos."

I went on listening intensely to the music. I memorized tunes and riffs. My older sister took piano lessons. I learned "Chopsticks" but refused my parents' offer of lessons. I did not want to mess around plunking those endless, cornball repetitions. I wanted to be an instant child prodigy like Sugar Child Robinson, but I could only make hash on the keys. So instead of playing an instrument, I played the turntable.

Jazz excited me and made me feel good. The sexual feeling beguiled me, but I was too young to know what was happening. I just listened and listened, and was warmed by the music. I learned to hear nuances and musicianship, expanded my range and became more selective. I found a clerk in a record shop who shared my interest, a very pretty girl—alas, at least five years older than I. Damn it!

But I went into rapture when she told me I had good taste. Once she rubbed my shoulder when I said something clever, and I almost passed out. She special-ordered records for me and put me on to new things. She took me to the listening booth and put on George Shearing or Sarah Vaughan. I kept willing her to come into the booth with me so I could smell her perfume, maybe brush her arm and gaze into her brown eyes as she talked about the music. She never did, but I knew that jazz had something to do with my feeling for her. When I played the records at home, I would think about her. My fantasies expanded and I began to realize that, as much as anything, jazz was about sex.

But I was a good Catholic boy and well brought up. In our house we had a copy of *Seven Storey Mountain,* Thomas Merton's autobiography of his young manhood and entry into Trappist life. Merton, too, loved jazz when he was a young, secular man, but he made a solemn and deliberate decision to give it up in order to realize his religious destiny. Was jazz evil? I did not understand why Merton had to do this. I knew I could never be that holy.

I was aware that jazz musicians drank a lot and took drugs. I had seen drunken people, but never a drug addict that I knew of. Apparently drugs relaxed them and helped them play better. The jazz life was intense and stressful. I knew that Gene Krupa had been arrested and sent to prison for taking drugs. I was aware that other musicians had problems. Schiavone's brother told me that Charlie Parker was a genius, but also a junkie. Occasionally articles in *Downbeat* hinted that certain musicians were having trouble.

I knew that marijuana was prevalent and that heroin was stronger and more dangerous. Someone told me that many of the big stars were on it. I could not visualize such an evil connected with this happy, sophisticated music. It was a world so far from my own. I studied their photographs and saw no traces of dissipation. They all looked clear-eyed and focused to me, not like the drunks I had seen slopping around. If drugs and alcohol made jazz musicians happy and helped them play music that I loved—well, then it was a sad business, but I guessed it was cool. I would sneak a mouthful of bourbon sometimes when my parents were out of the house. It was worse than medicine, but I got it down and could feel the buzz. It helped me understand the problem, and, yes, sometimes it made the jazz sound more interesting.

Every time I thought about jazz being improvised, it astonished me. I knew that painters painted over their work until they got it right, writers rewrote to perfect their stuff, singers and classical musicians performed from prepared scores, but jazz musicians put it down right on the spot. It went from their heads right out through the bells of their horns, the strings and skins of their instruments, the keys of the piano. This seemed very brave to me, almost a higher art. I forgave them their small indiscretions. No wonder they needed a little help once in a while. I figured if they died young, they were martyrs for their art.

I recall my amazement the first time I heard someone I respected refer to jazz musicians as "artists." I thought artists were people who painted, or who were writers, or singers in the Metropolitan Opera productions we listened to on Saturdays. Artists were serious, highly cultured adult people. My aunt was an artist and made some of her living doing etchings and colored drawings for Catholic prayer books. I admired her a great deal. But my aunt, or Ernest Hemingway, or Risë Stevens, or José Iturbe, seemed far removed from the jazz musicians I admired. Still, jazz musicians were artists, too, nocturnal artists who played in bars and smoky clubs, not generally appreciated or understood, artists who sometimes altered their consciousness in order to achieve something—but artists nevertheless.

In high school I endured study halls by making lists of musicians for dream jazz bands. I thought if I ever got rich I would bring these guys together to play. I must have looked studious as I worked on my enormous sections, which included a broad spectrum of boppers and swing players and even a few Dixielanders. I wanted everything. I made up these lists, over and over, and they looked something like this:

Tenor Sax	*Alto Sax*	*Trumpet*
Lester Young	Charlie Parker	Dizzy Gillespie
Flip Phillips	Benny Carter	Roy Eldridge
Stan Getz	Willie Smith	Louis Armstrong
Coleman Hawkins	Johnny Hodges	Buck Clayton
Chu Berry	Sonny Stitt	Sweets Edison
Georgie Auld	Lee Konitz	Miles Davis
Ben Webster		Harry James
Illinois Jacquet	*Baritone Sax*	Cootie Williams
Brew Moore	Harry Carney	Cat Anderson
Wardell Gray	Gerry Mulligan	Maynard Ferguson
Bud Freeman	Serge Chaloff	Red Allen
Don Byas	Bob Gioga	Howard McGhee

And so on through the trombonists, clarinetists, bassists, drummers. To pick a piano player I listed Bud Powell, Thelonious Monk, Teddy Wilson, Oscar Peterson, Mary Lou Williams, Al Haig, Art Tatum, George Shearing, and Erroll Garner. I could not decide which player I preferred, so figured I would just have a bunch of pianos put on the stage and let them all wail. It would be spectacular.

It was going to be a *big* band, and it was a contest to see who would be the leader. I considered Count Basie, Duke Ellington, Stan Kenton, and Woody Herman. Then I decided to bring them all in and alternate them. Four sets to a concert. It would take all night, but no one would go home. There were a lot of musicians, but I wanted a big, full sound, and I knew that Basie, Ellington, Kenton, and Herman could devise ways to make all these stars play together. I heard the huge band cooking in my mind as I made up my lists. Sometimes the study hall teacher would ask me to stop tapping my foot.

When adults asked me what I wanted to be when I grew up, I usually said I wanted to be a doctor. People were generally impressed with this and it would end the conversation. But I had no clue about my future. I knew I did not have the talent or the patience to be a jazz musician, but perhaps I could be some kind of artist. I took art classes in high school. Perhaps I could make a lot of money like Norman Rockwell and then bring my band together. The art teacher, intrusive and more than slightly inept, was Maude Rose. Her teaching technique was "hands-on." She took the brush out of your hand when you were working and smeared it around on your painting to show what you *should* be doing.

But I got off on the right foot with her. For the first lesson she wanted us to create small sculptures using ordinary objects. I had the idea of using peanuts and pipe cleaners to create jazz musician figures and shaped bits of tin foil into their horns. I made a conga drum out of a thimble and a little stage out of a shoebox. I rigged up some curtains stripped from a torn shirt and called it *Jam Session*. It was cool, and everyone admired it.

The next project was to do a drawing, not from life, but from our imaginations. I drew some musicians having a jam session. It was stilted and sloppy. I erased a lot, but Maude Rose said okay. I was hardly a talented student, but she had to move things along.

Finally, we were to do a watercolor, and, of course, I started to paint a jam session. I worked intensely, trying to get some feeling of improvisation into it. Other students painted flowers or landscapes, but I wanted to make a more personal expression.

Maude was touring the room, going from student to student, checking the work. When she came to mine she snorted, grabbed the brush out of my hand, and smeared a big X through my work. I stood up. "What are you *doing?*"

"You can't do any more jazz musicians," she said. "You've got to think of something else." She kept smearing the brush around, dipping it in the water, obliterating what I had done. I snatched the brush back out of her hand and accidentally bumped her so that she staggered back.

"Out!" she cried. "Get out!'

I was an inarticulate teenager, enraged, but helpless to express my anger at her rudeness.

"Out!" she shrieked again and gave me a push. I thought about pushing back, but, thank God, kept my hands to myself.

Oh, but I paid and paid anyway for this episode. Maude Rose gave me a big red F for the class. The principal told me that no one had ever failed art in the history of the school. My parents were undone. I was a dreamy, less than mediocre student anyway—but now to fail art? When they heard my explanation, they cut off my jazz records again. So I too was a martyr for jazz.

But no one could stop me from loving it. I took my jazz records with me to college and eventually found a compatible dorm roommate, Butterball Clark, who listened with me. Both of us were big on Stan Kenton, a dominant figure at the time. We would turn up those huge, brassy numbers on his 45 changer and beefed-up speakers, and people would be pounding on our door. Not even the 1812 Overture coming at top volume from the beleaguered classical lovers in the next room could blow us away.

College did not interest me; I ignored my classes and was told to leave after a year. I took a series of ridiculous jobs until I was drafted into the army in 1954. There was not much jazz in Kentucky, where I went through the obligatory misery of basic training at Fort Knox. It was a lonely, difficult, jazz-starved time, but one Saturday when we were cleaning our barracks a radio was playing. An enlightened Louisville disk jockey slipped in the Stan Getz/Johnny Smith "Moonlight in Vermont" side between some country music numbers. I guess he thought he could get away with it because of the guitar. I stopped and leaned enraptured on my broom. Some guy made a move to change the station and I hollered at him. He did not much like being shouted at, since it was his radio, so he headed in my direction for a serious chat but was intercepted by a formidable guy from Detroit named Rosenkrantz. Rosenkrantz settled him down, then came over to me. Jazz lovers are sometimes like a secret society.

"Do you know who that was on the radio?" he asked.

"Stan Getz and Johnny Smith."

"Man," he said. "I have been looking for you. Let's go have a beer when this party's over, and we can talk some sounds. I thought I was going to lose my mind with all these geetars and people singing through their noses."

During my army years, I was sent to Fort Slocum, New York, on an island off New Rochelle, for special training. After duty hours I taught myself how to travel into Manhattan and make my way to Fifty-second Street and the legendary jazz clubs. I went to the city almost every night, blowing my meager paychecks on cover charges, draught beer, and jazz. It was a dreamlike, glorious time.

The first time I did this, I was uncertain on the train and on the streets of New York. I walked up Pennsylvania Avenue from the station with a map of Manhattan in my hand. Above all else, I wanted to find Birdland. I turned on Fifty-second and walked into the District—Basin Street, the Open Door, Three Deuces—and just around the corner and down the street on

Broadway there were the Royal Roost, the Band Box, and, beside it, the awning and sign of Birdland, "The Jazz Corner of the World." The billboard in front read in block letters:

BUD POWELL TRIO
SYLVIA SYMS

When I paid the cover charge, my hand was shaking. I shyly declined a waiter's offer to take me to a table and was directed to the listener's gallery along the left side of the bandstand. I was early and got a good seat beside a pillar, right up against the railing beside the stage. A recording of "Salt Peanuts" was blowing on the sound system. I ordered a beer and studied the women in the gathering crowd.

The lights dimmed and Peewee Marquette came out on the stage in his little tuxedo and made one of his strident announcements. Marquette, a midget, was hugely proud of his position as emcee at Birdland. He felt it was his serious duty to keep things moving along. To the great irritation of musicians, he would often interject himself at the end of sets before they finished playing. I read later that Lester Young used to call him "half a motherfucker."

Peewee cranked the microphone down. "Ladies and gentlemen, Birdland is taking a great deal of pride at this time to present to you the very wonderful Bud Powell and his trio. How about a little welcome for the Bud Powell Trio!" We applauded, Marquette left the stage, and then there was a pause. A long pause.

Finally, the kitchen door opened at the right side of the stage, breaking the darkness. Three figures emerged. One of them, a huge black man, guided a smaller man across the stage to the piano with firm hands on his shoulders. It was Charlie Mingus leading Bud Powell, who sat down on the bench and slumped over the keys with his eyes half closed. Mingus went to his bass and picked it up. He nodded to the drummer as he watched Powell carefully. The drummer started brushing a medium tempo; then Mingus began plucking his strings. He kept his eyes on Powell. The drummer kept his eyes on Powell. We all kept our eyes on Powell, wondering what would happen. Suddenly, Bud lifted his head and brought his hands down to strike a chord on the keys. Then, amazingly, he was bouncing into "Audrey." Soon he was sweating and ranting as he played. It was a wonderful set. I remember lovely versions of "My Heart Stood Still" and "Polka Dots and Moonbeams," the march into the strange "Glass Enclosure," his Bachian introduction to the beguiling "Sure Thing," and a breakneck "I Want to Be Happy."

The legend was bouncing before my eyes—and the legends continued to roll. I went into the city frequently taking the early-evening train so I could get a good seat. It was a golden, privileged period of my life. In those clubs I heard a large portion of the galaxy: Coleman Hawkins, Lester Young, Don Byas, Hank Mobley, Thelonious Monk, Sarah Vaughan, Carmen McRae, Gerry Mulligan, Erroll Garner, Oscar Peterson, Stan Getz, Dexter Gordon, Dizzy Gillespie, Roy Eldridge, Zoot Sims, Milt Jackson, Oscar Pettiford, Ray Brown, Al Cohn, Chet Baker, Max Roach, Art Blakey, Buddy Rich, Terry Gibbs, Phineas Newborn, Sonny Stitt, Buddy De Franco, Tony Scott, George Shearing, Art Tatum, Teddy Wilson, Lee Konitz, Charlie Shavers, Miles Davis. They even stuffed whole big bands—Basie, Ellington, Kenton, Herman—onto those small stages. They literally blew you away in those little clubs.

One blessed late spring evening I walked down Fifty-second and turned the corner onto Broadway, reading the billboards as I made my way. It was glorious license to be able to pick your pleasure from those offered riches. I stopped at the entrance to Basin Street when I saw these words:

CHARLIE PARKER
ELLA FITZGERALD

I went to my pocket and got my dough out fast.

Of course, I was early and got a good seat. I was tremendously excited about hearing Bird, so stirred up I do not remember hearing Ella Fitzgerald. I cannot even recall who played in the rhythm sections, but then Bird came out and joined the other musicians. He was wearing a powder-blue serge suit and suede shoes. I knew the legends of his dissipation, but he seemed keen and bright-eyed. He played magnificently, crisp and clean, no fluffing or wavering, but soaring as he did on my old Verve and Dial waxes back in Ohio. I was captivated. What I did not know was that he was in his last months, a brief period of clarity before the abrupt, final descent. Three months later he attempted suicide. Nine months later he was dead. I am very grateful for what I heard.

I was at Camp Desert Rock in Nevada when Solomon Womble told me he'd heard that Bird had died. I found it hard to believe. When I listened to him play that night he had seemed the most adult person in the world. I look now at his photographs, the stages of his short life, and the astonishing variety of his appearance. Sometimes he looked like a young pug, sometimes a businessman, a driven artist, a Buddha, a happy clown, and, yes, sometimes a haunted, wide-eyed junkie. Charlie Parker was thirty-four years old when he died. As I write this, I am more than thirty years older than he was when he passed, but I will never live to be as old as he was.

An ephemeral, sprightly strain of jazz called "West Coast" became briefly prominent in the mid and late 1950s. I collected and listened fervently to this jazz, generally produced on bright, transparent 45 records with artsy album covers. It is common to patronize this music, and I must admit that I rarely listen to it now. But in the mid-1950s—the middle of the Eisenhower years—it came like sunlight and warm breezes into those dreary Ohio winters, brightening my uncertain days, making me dream of being warm and free on the California beaches. It was pat, but clever and effervescent, usually swinging hard, the tunes frequently titled with puns like "The Sweetheart of Sigmund Freud," "Coming through the Rye Bread," "Coop de Graas."

While I was stationed at Desert Rock, several of us decided to take a pass and drive to Los Angeles for a few days. I was not thinking about jazz. We took a room on Redondo Beach, put on shorts, and started strolling south along the sand—three girl-starved guys walking the beach. There was plenty of sand at Desert Rock, but not this kind of sand, and I had never seen such glorious flesh, so many delectable women.

When we reached Hermosa Beach, I looked up the street into the town and there was Howard Rumsey's Lighthouse Café, a mecca of West Coast jazz. I could not believe my eyes. I dragged my pals away from their girl watching and up the sidewalk to check it out. It was Saturday and an afternoon session was scheduled. I was ecstatic, irresistible in my powers of persuasion. We paid the cover charge and went in, bought a round of beers, and sat at the bar. By the time the musicians came in I was crocked, but I remember Bob Cooper, Richie Kamuca, Bob Brookmeyer, Shorty Rogers, Rumsey, and Stan Levy.

These were the *guys*. When they tuned up and sailed into their first number, I was enraptured, young, happy, and very drunk. Here it was—California jazz life as I had dreamed about it in my bedroom back in Ohio with my 45 changer spinning. "Warm Breeze," "Surf Ride," "Didi."

By that time in my life, I had decided I wanted to be a poet. Listening to jazz has always made me feel "poetic." I was tremendously excited. I kept asking the bartender for pencil and paper. I wanted to make notes and sketch a few lines on the spot. He ignored me.

My buddies were looking at the women, as I was, but I was grooving on the music too. Nobody was feeling the whole thing like I was. Here was the life of the artist, the freedom and decadence. Finally my friends wanted to get back to the beaches. I wouldn't leave, and they left me there. I stayed the rest of the afternoon and finished hearing the set. I had a hamburger and french fries, took a walk and sobered up a little, then hung around for the evening set and started all over. By closing time I was a mess, but somehow I found my way back to our room.

When Suzanne and I married in 1959, we hauled my jazz records with us to California in our 1952 Chevrolet. We settled in San Francisco for a while and got jobs. We were finished with school and enjoying our young lives. In the evenings and on weekends, we roamed the city. We got into the Blackhawk to hear Dave Brubeck, Cal Tjader, and others. At a wonderful bar called the Hangover we listened to Earl Hines and Muggsy Spanier. In North Beach was a joint called the Jazz Workshop where we took in Ben Webster, Sonny Rollins, Jimmy Witherspoon, the Modern Jazz Quartet, Hampton Hawes, Rahsaan Roland Kirk, and others.

I had been working hard on my poems. In the mid-1960s I started to get acceptances from magazines and gained some confidence. We moved to Los Angeles, where I managed the UCLA bookstore. I noticed a guy who kept coming into the store to check out the poetry section and struck up a conversation with him. He was a Unitarian minister named Jim Daniels, and we fell in together, started taking lunch once a week to talk about poetry and jazz.

The Watts riots ignited in 1966, and we were all disturbed, feeling guilty and worried. Jim kept encouraging me to write about it. He wanted to create an arts event dealing with Watts, to raise awareness in the people who attended his lily-white church in the San Fernando Valley. I knew nothing about Watts, but I knew how I felt about racism. I was young and hopeful that I might be able to do some good, so I worked at a few poems about slavery, prejudice, and racial anger. They were poems of the moment, immature and overly dramatic, but Daniels showed them to a music teacher in his congregation, and the guy took them to some of his jazz musician friends.

The next time I had lunch with Daniels, he told me he had arranged to have an event in his church, that some musicians were working up music to go with my poems, and I would be the reader at the performance. The first rehearsal would be the following week. I was excited but intimidated; up to that point I had only read poems out loud to Suzanne and a few friends.

"Duck soup," he said. "You'll be great."

"Who are the musicians?" I asked.

He took a piece of paper out of his pocket and read, "Hampton Hawes on piano, Teddy Edwards tenor, Ralph Pena bass, and Shelly Manne on drums."

"Lord, have mercy!" I gasped. I was in way over my head. These were musicians I revered. I owned their albums and looked at their pictures. I had no business being on the same stage with them. I worried and fussed for a week, and Suzanne did her best to buck me up.

"Those guys are like gods," I told her. "I'm going to make an ass of myself. I can't do this."

"Then make a very good ass of yourself," she said. "Onward."

The rehearsal was in a big meeting room next to the church. I was tingling and short of breath as I lumbered across the parking lot. The musicians had already arrived and were tuning up. Jim Daniels took me by the sleeve and walked me over to them. They looked up and smiled engagingly, those faces so familiar to me. Each of them stood up and shook my hand warmly.

I was in another dimension—a little boy babbling in front of his heroes. My hands were shaking and my voice was high. The only thing I could think to say was, "I'm proud to be doing this with you guys. I think your work is great."

Teddy Edwards put down his horn and gave me a gentle poke on the arm. Hampton Hawes—the Hampton Hawes who had played with Charlie Parker, Dexter Gordon, Wardell Gray, Art Pepper, Sonny Rollins—grinned handsomely. "Hey, man," he said, "we really dig your work too."

Winter

Fear no more the heat o' the sun,
Nor the furious winter's rages.
Thou thy worldly task has done,
Home art gone and ta'en thy wages.

Shakespeare, *Cymbeline*

By the time we finished moving all our possessions to the driftless hills, the year had turned and it was hard winter. I was pleased with our new freedom, but it would take a long time to make at least a partial recovery from my abrupt retirement. It is inevitable that the cold heaviness of winter can bear you down on occasion, and I was carrying a considerable load. But winter was the perfect time to make this transition.

I know how to act in the presence of the muse, have been preparing all my adult life for this cohabitation. Every morning Sheba and I walk to the writing shack and work as long as we wish. She perches on a rug on top of a table and gives me full reports on any deer or turkeys that have the temerity to wander out of the woods into our fields.

Eskimos have many words for snow. That winter, some of them were defined for us, but we never stopped walking out in

the fields and woods. Walking is our panacea. It heals in all
weather. I especially like strolling in mounting snow, pure
whiteness, no wind interfering with its light spirals until the
temperature rises slightly and the flakes twirl down in large
clusters. If I were to name these snows, I would call them "Wet
plumes."

There are, of course, fierce snows as well, after dark the
inches mounting quickly, blowing, drifting, and bitter. Sometimes in a winter night the world seems like the inside of a
mausoleum. I would call these snows "Winterreise" after
Schubert's great melancholy song cycle.

There are frigid, blustery nights when even Sheba hesi-
tates before going out the door, and she has the heavy long
hair of a bearded collie. We can persuade her to go only a few
yards beyond the library, where she squats briefly for her
business, then dashes back in out of the frigid wind to sit the
rest of the evening beside the fireplace. John Crowe Ransom
wrote of the furious winter night blowing "a cry of Absence,
Absence, in the heart"—and so these snows could be called
"Absence."

Once, after several days of mounting snow, the weather
cleared and it grew sunny; then the temperature dropped
again, freezing a hard crust on top. When we walked on this it
resounded as if we were stepping on old roof tiles, or walking
across a glass skylight. Sheba had a tough time. She stepped
mincingly like a ballerina to stay on top, but if she tried to run
or bound she fell through, and her legs grew sore from the
scraping. The crust was at least half an inch thick and pebbled.
When we dislodged pieces with our boots, they slid down the
slopes a long way, making a rumbling sound until they butted
up against tree trunks. The sun melted the snow in the
branches, and when it refroze, the light glinted in facets of ice
like fine chandeliers.

I recall a day when there was a thin powder of snow on top of ice in the woods. We could not keep our feet, and I slid crashing spread-eagle up against a tree. Suzanne fell and bumped her head. Even Sheba was scrabbling. When we were younger such conditions would have amused us, but they are hazardous to aging people. We crawled up the slope on our hands and knees, and shuffled along the road, retreating to the house. This kind of snow requires an ominous name like "Hip-cracker."

The best snows are no more than six inches, wet snows that plaster the trees and make etchings of the branches. There is only light wind, so everything is quiet in black and white. For a contrast, some crows squat on scrawny thinned-out trees, bending them down and swaying them. I call these snows "Dürer."

We were amazed one moderate day in this fresh country place to see soot on the snow. Suzanne and I remember from our childhoods snow turning gray in the mill towns. Looking closely, we saw that the black spots had small antennae and were jumping and moving. It was not soot. We ran to our insect guides. Springtails. Richie Halverson calls them snow fleas. Under certain conditions they hatch in sunlight on the snow and appear in legions; I can't tell if they are breeding or warring with each other. They hop like microscopic frogs, are like gunpowder or living soot. They fall into our boot marks, their masses shading the prints because they are unable to hop out. I have not yet determined the purpose of these strange winter creatures, but I am relieved to know they are not real fleas.

On clear winter nights I sometimes rise from bed and gaze from our living room window at moonlight on the spread of snow. It stretches all the way across the valley to the next ridge, stippled with farm lights. Everything near and far is sparkling—the snow, the stars in the night sky, even the frozen crystals in the drifts on our deck.

If the temperature rises during the night, a fog comes up the slopes and lingers in the snowy woods until late morning; it is as if we were strolling through milk. If the sky is clear above the fog layer, the sunlight is muted on the snow and trees, creating a chill, mysterious, marblized landscape. When the fog is thin and the sun shows through it, it seems like the core of perfect whiteness—the whitest white in the world, containing all other colors. If there were a hoary spirit of winter, a resurrection of a Norse god, this would be his scene. When the fog begins to break, it rises and thins; sometimes there are openings through the vapor into the blue.

If snow cover lasts more than a week on the ground without additional accumulation, there is a veritable traffic jam of tracks. When we arrived in the driftless hills, we were enchanted to discover how many winter animal and bird neighbors live here. They are numerous and obscure, but they leave traces of themselves: the precise, knucklelike prints of deer; raccoon claws; tentative spaced-out scribbles of rabbits; nervous checking of turkeys; coyote heel and half moon toes; the prints of foxes, dogs, small and large birds. The vulnerable little stitches of mice and the tunnels of voles sometimes run all the way out to the center of the fields. We wonder why they feel such perilous trips are necessary. There are sometimes abrupt, stark wing imprints where hawks or owls swoop in to terminate these imprudent journeys.

We found a dead, old raccoon in the snow about ten feet out of the woods one morning. It looked as if its sides and the scruff of its neck had been scourged by talons. Blood had jetted from its mouth and its legs were splayed. I doubt that it ever had a chance against its enemy, perhaps a large owl, dropping from above. Nothing had been eaten—it was as if the attacker was simply testing its mettle.

There are feathery marks where grouse slant down on the fresh powder to make delicate landings like seraphim. Through all of this winter season I brooded on my betrayal. The memories visited me night and day, and took portions of my spirit. But it restored me to realize that now I live in a place where angels descend and make their gentle marks in the snow.

The Condition of My Faith

There lives more faith in honest doubt,
Believe me, than in half the creeds.

Alfred, Lord Tennyson, *In Memoriam*

A JEWISH RABBI FRIEND surprised me twenty-five years
ago, after we had spent several pleasantly ardent hours dis-
cussing literature and art. As if this were a natural progression,
he asked, "And what is the condition of your faith?" I realized
he had been setting me up for this throughout the afternoon.
He was a social friend, a fellow writer, and I am not Jewish—
but, after all, this was his work. At the conclusion of our
afternoon of high talk, it was an amicable question, and he was
assuming I had some faith to condition. The bumptious old
comic strip character Major Hoople used to go "Awk, guff,
mumble, whiff!" when he was caught in an uneasy position.
That's what I did. I tried to dazzle the rabbi with footwork—
but he knew. I could only shuffle and equivocate. My faith had
been breathing hard and in bad condition for a long time.

It hasn't improved much since. On rare occasions when I
attend a religious service, even now as they are modernized
and made contemporary with lay readings and guitar music,

my old feelings of disdain for the superficiality return. Public
displays of righteousness have always appalled me, and they
seem to me more than ever like empty, overwrought displays.
When I was a young man I savored the arch little poems of
Stephen Crane:

What?
You define me God with these trinkets?
Can my misery meal on an ordered walking
Of surpliced numbskulls?
And a fanfare of lights?
Or even upon the measured pulpitings
Of the familiar false and true?
Is this God?
Where, then, is hell?
Show me some bastard mushroom
Sprung from a pollution of blood.
It is better.

How did I come to such a condition? I started out zealously
as an ardent Roman Catholic boy, taking solidly to the ancient
catechism stampeded by the priests and nuns. I recall my
Uncle Junie, just back from hard experiences in World War II,
expressing doubts and arguing with my mother about religion.
He worried that he was losing his faith, and my mother criti-
cized his wavering. I was in first grade, looking forward to my
first communion, infused with piety and greatly agitated by
the argument. I wanted to reinforce her. She *was* my mom. At
one point, when Junie expressed difficulty in believing that the
consecrated Eucharist was actually the body of Christ, I
stepped in, declaring that I believed in this mystery even
though I didn't understand it. He should just do the same. My
mother hugged me and stroked my righteous little swan neck.
"You see, Junie," she said. "This is blind faith. This is what you
should have." My uncle looked at me coldly, then went off to

smoke a cigarette. I was sorry I had crossed him. I admired him enormously and wanted to impress him. He remained a Catholic, married in the church, and had four children, while I am the one who lost the mysteries.

Something happened—or, rather, some things happened. For instance, I prepared assiduously for that first communion. I was six years old and, beyond birthdays and Christmases, this was the first big event in my life. I was very nervous and wanted to do everything perfectly. The nuns were all business. Their strictness terrorized me. If my mind wandered—and I was a copious daydreamer—they whacked my knuckles with a ruler. Each day we went to the church and practiced singing and processionals. We drilled catechism relentlessly.

Father Gallagher came once a week to our classroom. The desk seats clattered on their hinges as we shot up in unison, shouting, "Good morning, Father!" He would pop questions about our studies, always saving a few important ones for last. "Now, children, here is a big question. I'll give a dime to anyone who can answer it. What is the meaning of the commandment 'Thou shalt not take the name of the Lord thy God in vain'?" Hands shot into the air. Bobby Gaum, the most prolific cusser on the playground, was called on. He said, "It means you shouldn't swear, Father," and he got the dime. I was shy, generally uncertain, and never got the money. If it was a really tough question, usually one of the girls gave the right answer—the ubiquitous Loretta Donohue or sometimes Bernadette Malone, whose brother was a priest.

The nuns instructed us rigorously on receiving the Eucharist. At the altar rail we were to close our eyes, lift our heads, open our mouths, and stick out our tongues so that the priest could lay the communion wafers on them. We were told emphatically not to chew the Host, but let it dissolve on our tongues, not even permitting our teeth to come into contact

with it. We were to return to our pews, kneel with our heads
in our hands held in prayer, and speak to God in this new
intimacy.

We would be holding the body of Christ in our mouths,
and the responsibility crushed down on my six-year-old soul.
I wasn't sure I wanted to eat a body—least of all the Lord's.
What would a body taste like? Even though I had blind faith,
I worried a good deal about this procedure. I pressed slices of
Bond bread flat and cut out circles with a bottle cap so I could
practice. I tried to let them melt on my tongue, but I always
choked and ended up chewing and swallowing.

My parents bought me the requisite white suit. There is a
snapshot taken after the communion mass: I am standing in
our backyard on a bench in my immaculate suit, looking very
serious and bony—I had been sick most of the year with
bronchial infections. Usually I looked directly at the camera
and smiled when my picture was snapped, but in this photograph my head is turned and I am staring off with a guilty
look, the demeanor of a boy who feels doomed. I had reason
to be concerned.

I worried throughout the long, hot, solemn high mass. I
tried to pray, but the words were like gritty pebbles in my
mouth. We had fasted for the communion and the heavy
incense from the censers made me feel slightly ill. I coughed a
great deal. At last we filed to the altar rail and knelt. I closed
my eyes and listened uneasily as Father Gallagher approached
down the line of communicants toward me, bearing the chal-
ice full of Hosts. At last he came to me and I raised my head as
he placed the body of Christ on my tongue. The organ was
playing joyously and the choir was singing. I knew the eyes of
my parents and older sister were on me.

I was gagging as I returned to the pew. I knelt and put my
head in my hands, my eyes watering as I choked. I gave enor-

mous effort, trying not to let the Host touch my teeth, but at last I retched and it dropped from my mouth. Apparently no one saw; my mates were dealing with their own responsibilities. I peered down through the cavern of my folded hands at the small circle of leavened bread—Christ's body—on the filthy floorboards of the church, just in front of the kneeling bench. It seemed like a peephole into white-hot Hades.

The ceremony continued and I prayed to God, not in our new intimacy, but out of fear, asking him to forgive me and not allow anyone to see what I had done. At the end of the mass we rose in procession and walked singing past our adoring families. I mouthed the words. I could not meet the eyes of my parents. Instead I stole worried glances at the nuns, studying their expressions, hoping they would not notice the small white circle under the pew where I had been sitting and thereby determine who had perpetrated this monstrous sin. The horror filled me. I could not imagine the punishment for such a thing. Other than murder, it seemed the worst possible sin. The nuns had told us that when a priest accidentally dropped a Host, it had to be covered with a consecrated cloth and later ceremoniously retrieved. The priest then had to spend many hours in penance for his clumsiness.

For a long time I wondered what had happened to the Host on the grimy church floor. My best hope was that it had been discovered and had a consecrated cloth placed over it, and that priests had prayed for the wretched soul who had gagged it out. But perhaps the janitors had swept it up without noticing, and the body of Christ was stuck to garbage in some dump. I tried not to think about my burning in hell throughout eternity.

The look on my face in the photograph bears witness to my very private guilt. I confessed to no one—not my parents, the nuns, or Father Gallagher. I was not certain what the future held. My *first* communion. What a terrible beginning—but I kept my burden to myself. I look at this photograph sixty years later and still feel a twinge of culpability.

A few years ago, a nun enthusiastically brought her high school creative writing class to one of my poetry readings. Her being in the audience made me slightly nervous, but I included some writings about my early difficulties with Catholicism and the harsh treatment I had received at the hands of the sisters when I was young. The audience, and the nun's students, thought the stories were hilarious. She even chuckled a bit herself. Afterwards, in a showy display of compunction, I went to where she sat. "I'm sorry," I said. "I hope I haven't offended you."

"That's fine," she said. "No problem. Things have changed since you were young, and most people know this. Your poems are very funny."

That should have been enough, but I persisted in my show of overwrought contrition. "I didn't mean to show you up in front of your students."

"Oh, we get used to it," she said. "It's easy enough to make fun of us."

Awk, guff, mumble, whiff. Whack, went the ruler on my knuckles—even after all the years.

I am glad things have changed since I was a child. But a residue of guilt and fear remain. There were many pressures. We had a saint in the family, and that bore down heavily on me, too. Dode Wigand, a distant cousin to my father, was an older man who had been sickly since he was a child. Dode devoted himself to holiness. The whole family deferred to his piety. To a grade-schooler, his life seemed to be mostly prayer and naps, although he did take some time out to watch baseball. But Dode was a holy man.

I never understood what his physical problem was—a series of strokes, I believe—but he had little energy and spent a great deal of time lying on a cot in a room set up for him downstairs in his family's large house. When we went to see the Wigands, usually on Sundays after church, Dode rarely noticed me, but when he did he was kindly, taking me onto his lap, giving me little prayer cards and unusual medals to pin to my shirt. But his proximity frightened me. His sickly face came close to mine and I could see the white whiskers in his pallid skin, the veins in his red eyes, the dampness of his nostrils. Once he gave me a card with a picture of Christ knocking at a door. On the other side of the door was a young man seated at a desk stacked with books, looking up pensively from a page. The door was central to the picture, dark colored and hinting at possibilities. Would the young man hear the knock, the call to the priesthood?

There was a holy-water font in the doorway of Dode's room and on each wall elaborate crucifixes garlanded with palm leaves. The tables were filled with missals, breviaries, and prayer books. Dode had been unable to answer the call; nevertheless, he had devoted himself and found holiness. He did not go to priests—they regularly came to him for spiritual nourishment. Family members and friends came into his room at least twice a day to pray and say the rosary with him.

He had lots of sisters. Some of them might have been married, but they all seemed like nuns to me, ministresses and witnesses to his faith. They appeared to be in perpetual adoration, as in pictures I had seen of Saint Agnes and Saint Veronica.

Dode had one of the first commercial television sets. The screen was round, and he watched broadcasts of Sunday masses from the cathedral in Cleveland; in the afternoons, when he was feeling less ecclesiastical, he sometimes gazed at primitive productions of Cleveland Indians games. The set was art deco, like an elaborate tabernacle with a round hole to expose the Host. Even this seemed to flicker with holy light.

He had the authority and dedication of a man who had prepared all his life for death and salvation. Everything in that large house was "religious," and it was like a citadel church itself. It sat up from a pretty lake, and on Sunday afternoons a gathering of fundamentalists, wrapped in white sheets, came to the shores below the house and baptized in the shallows. They made a lot of noise and were ghostly, enthusiastic, and terrifying to a little kid as they dipped each other back into the water. Hallelujah! I sat with Dode amid the cluster of my family on the Wigands' porch, and we watched silently from our high Catholicism. It seemed a long way down to this primeval display.

I don't remember how and when Dode finally died, but when my parents told me he had passed on I *knew* that he had at last been borne to heaven by angels. There never seemed to be a moment of doubt among the Wigands. Their spirituality was secure, and the saint in their house defined it. Dode's high example was a load for me: having a saint in the family complicated my already challenged grade school life. His precedent was something to distantly hope for, even to brag about to my mates and teachers, but secretly I hoped I would never feel compelled to be that holy.

I was the only Catholic kid in our neighborhood. It seemed unlikely—in fact, it seemed downright nasty and un-Christian of me to believe—that my non-Catholic friends were going to have to do time in limbo or were damned to eternal hell because they lacked "the true faith." When the time came for me to go to high school, my parents allowed me my choice. Over protests, threats, and dire warnings from priests and nuns, I decided to attend a public school rather than Central Catholic. I was not a very successful young person, but the experiences of youth and young manhood, the variety of companionship, the realization that there are reasonable alternatives and pleasures in the world, took effect.

I went on to try and fail at college, then worked for a year in a steel mill. When I was drafted into the army I was assigned with some hundreds of young soldiers to witness the atomic explosions in Nevada from positions close to ground zero. The force and devastation we experienced remain with me always.

The drill was desperate and we had no choice. Camp Desert Rock in winter was a cold, gray place descending to darkness. There was nothing to cheer us or elevate our spirits. Nights when we were not on maneuvers we guzzled beer in the post exchange or stared numbly at bad movies in a chilly Quonset hut. No one could convince me that God was there. Any God I could have believed in would not have been responsible for my being in such a place.

A tough, old, hard-drinking priest named Father Tucker came in once a week from an air force base to say mass for the Catholic soldiers. He sometimes accompanied us in our movements under the boiling mushroom clouds to witness the destruction. He was a bleak man and, lacking our buffer of guileless youth, was driven to further desolation by what he saw. I believe he, too, sensed that God was not present at Camp Desert Rock or at the rote little masses he hurriedly celebrated. I sometimes attended his services, held in a dismal tin shack near the officers' club.

One weary, hopeless Sunday, when he gave his sermon with an obviously painful hangover, he wretchedly claimed that he had no sacramental wine for the communion because someone had stolen the bottle from his car. He faltered and stumbled during the mass. At one point he suddenly turned to us from the altar, his voice staggering and eyes pouring. I had never seen such desolation. To my young eyes, he seemed near death.

He confessed that he was not good. He said that, being there, none of us were good. It was impossible for anyone to be good in such a place. He said he was a failure in the face of evil, had no right to stand before us as our priest.

The few of us were dumbfounded. Although we were too unseasoned to realize it, all of us at that moment, including Father Tucker, had reached a turning point in our spiritual lives. None of us was likely ever to forgive our being put in that malevolent place, or what it had done to us.

In a few moments Father Tucker regained himself. Like a good soldier, he took hold and turned away from his handful of confessors to finish his mass.

After my army service, when I was twenty-three, I fell in love with a beautiful young woman who had been raised a Lutheran. Suzanne and I loved each other and spent too much time arguing religion when we could have been dancing and laughing. Churches have become more ecumenical and tolerant, but in those days the division was strict and the boundaries were militantly guarded. I was dutiful in my Catholicism and pushed hard, but she refused to take "instructions" in the Catholic faith, and of course she refused to out-and-out agree to allow our children to be raised Catholics. She didn't push Lutheranism, but suggested other reasonable possibilities. The big moral question I faced was whether I would marry "out of the church."

The priests leaned heavily on me. "But I love this woman," I told them, and they shrugged their shoulders. When I finally told Father Gallagher that we had decided to compromise and marry in an Episcopalian church, he turned the color of a cured ham. I asked him if I would *really* go to hell for marrying this woman I loved most deeply. He would not respond, would not give me an answer, would not take the responsibility of telling me I was doomed.

Onward to hell, then! The next Sunday I skipped mass and went with her to a Lutheran service, adding a huge black blotch to the sin that already tarnished and overwhelmed my darkening soul. We married and eventually I forgot about guilt. After some initial effort at a workable compromise, we fell away from organized religion completely and enjoyed the blessed ritual of our own Sunday mornings together—casual breakfasts, long walks in the woods, gardening, then later playing and camping out with our children. Four decades have passed, and we have not looked back. I'll trade eternity for them.

Eventually I couldn't believe in anything, and I am not sure what would have held my attention and faith. I wanted sure signs—proof of some kind of divinity. Flannery O'Connor, professing her belief in the Holy Eucharist, wrote in a letter that "if it's only a symbol, to hell with it." I lacked that kind of astonishing toughness and intensity. I wanted tangible demonstrations, wanted Aristotle's unmoved mover to come down like an anvil through the fan vaulting of the chancel, crack some of the scrubbed stones, and show himself on the altar. I wanted palpable, authenticated relics—bones, teeth, splinters. I wanted confirmed reports of prophets in the countryside. I wanted holy and powerful signs, symbols I could touch, instead of the mystic drone on the altar.

Sometimes I still try to pray; perhaps I lost my chance when the Host fell from my mouth. When I speak the words they seem rote and wooden, like saying you're sorry right after a bad fight with someone. A rosary seems as devotional and passionate as an old picket fence. When I try to make up my own prayers I am always asking for favors or seeking special dispensations for loved ones or myself. I end up begging, or I pray out of fear.

Father Tucker wept because he was not good, because goodness was not possible in that malignant place. What is goodness? Does it exist only in certain places and under certain conditions? I don't believe that goodness is the same thing Christian fundamentalists believe it is. Some people believe that ethnic cleansing is good. Some believe that possession of guns protects goodness.

So what do I think? Compassion. I believe that goodness is compassion. I can say this for certain. But there are people who believe that compassion is a weakness undermining the preservation and protection of a goodness they feel certain of. They make holy wars over this. The slaughter is appalling. Are such wars good? Why would a "supreme being" permit such things?

I still seek goodness—something to believe in. I have tried many things. I have no knowledge of great religious texts, though many times I have made lists and planned to read and contemplate the holy books: the Bible, the Talmud, the Ramayana, the Tao Te Ching, the I Ching, the Tripitaka, the Vedas, and other religious and moral texts. My sincerity was great, but my faith, resolve, and intelligence were weak. I began by sampling and superficially reading, but alas, my intent easily evaporated in the face of other duties and desires. What did I imagine I would gain from reading these texts? My mind and soul easily wandered as I looked at them. I had no context, no history or background.

The oppressive history of Roman Catholicism revolts and shames me. No wonder that at the turn of the millennium Pope John Paul took time to apologize for some things in the church's past, particularly its harassment of defectors and heretics, and for its anti-Semitism.

The historic residue of this persecution remains throughout the world. Our small house in Puivert is located in the south central section of France. The area is full of stark reminders of the hard, dominant historic Catholicism of earlier residents. Along the roadsides are antique shrines and statues of the crucified Christ, nailed up naked and sallow in the elements to remind wayfarers of the one true faith.

Near us the Cathédrale Sainte-Cécile, an imposing fortified church in Albi, is a prime example of religious power. It was begun late in the thirteenth century, about fifty years after the genocidal crusade against the Cathar heretics had concluded. It is a curious, accordion-like edifice with thirty-three loopholed towers, looking like rows of rockets, constituting the outside walls; a tall, battlemented bell tower rises at one end. The paintings and carvings inside the church are carefully preserved. In the choir are statues of the apostles and the prophets, modeled after rich local merchants who were heavy contributors to the church, and they are remarkable studies of medieval aristocrats. The vaults are ornately painted with decorations, symbols, angels, and other images—with Christ high in the center, a book of the Ten Commandments open like a visual aid on his lap, his hand raised in a teaching gesture.

But the most astonishing feature of the cathedral is the commanding painting of the Last Judgment surrounding the main altar—a grim reminder of what is in store for sinners and faltering Catholics. The representation is done in descending layers. At the top in ethereal clouds are the seraphim, cherubim, thrones, virtues, and archangels. On the next level down, the saints in heaven are lined up in a prayerful row, gold pie pans stuck to their heads. Below them are the saved in heaven—priests, monks, bishops, archbishops, a few nuns, and some pious, prosperous-looking aristocrats. Underneath them, on earth, are the righteous and devout, bearing books of Scripture. They are naked, praying and hopeful as they follow an angel toward the altar. In the next level are depicted the faltering and doubtful people, nude and holding their hands in

supplication, wading and struggling through a quagmire
toward possible salvation. One hopes that a few of them at
least still have a chance, because below them is hell itself,
almost at eye level for the congregation—a stunning depiction
of the damned writhing in a sea of lava, vomit, and feculence
as devils in various horrid forms torment them with chains,
prongs, racks, and garrotes, siccing monstrous creatures on
them to bite and maim. There are whores in a tub, riding
through flames and being speared by a scaled goat figure with
huge breasts. Gluttons are force-fed excrement. The avaricious
are boiled screaming in molten metal. The bad tempered are
restrained in white-hot chains and beaten with bastinadoes
and flails. The envious are scourged and disfigured by the
beaks of horrid creatures, half lizard, half bird. The proud are
racked on fiery wheels as devils flail their genitals. Everyone is
screaming and puking.

My hair stands on end even now as I think of it. The painting is *vivid*. What a tradition, what shameful history! It makes
Nazi propaganda seem like tea talk. Any ignorant scamp,
handed a sword and sent out to beat on heretics after being
threatened with such horrors, would be ready to chew up
scenery.

If I could connect now with an ancient faith, it would not be
one that had such a long history of subjugation. Perhaps I
could have been a faithful Etruscan two thousand years ago.
The names of their twenty-eight gods were inscribed on a
bronze, life-sized replica of a liver divided into zones or
"houses." Their priests studied the liver of a sacrificed animal,
noting irregularities of size or color or evidence of disease, and
then matched these signs to the zones on the bronze liver to
find which god was sending messages. Their universe was pan-
theistic and their gods dwelled in the macrocosm as well as in
microcosms like the sheep liver. Every bird, berry, turd, organ,

tree, and bowl of wine could be of significance. The critic
Lapos Fulep has said of Paul Cézanne, "The view of some
apples or some pieces of bacon produces a spiritual experience
as majestic as was, for Giotto, the tearful contemplation of the
Virgin during prayer." I am sure there was misery, doubt, fear,
and even guilt in Etruria, but at least the Etruscans must have
felt that they were always in proximity to a god.

I may seem craven, now that I have lived so much of my life
without religion, to concern myself with it again. Perhaps I will
regret this, but I have always been amused by tales of deathbed
conversions, people touching all the bases at the end. I envy
persons who have maintained faith—not the overbearing, self-
righteous ones, but those who have been quietly nurtured by
belief throughout their lives. They are most fortunate. It seems
that I should believe in *something*, but I believe only that it is
presumptuous for any individual or organization to claim possession of the main line on a "supreme being" or "the one true
faith."

I believe in art, believe that art is good. But I do *not* believe
in Frances Bacon's ruthless paintings of slabs of rotting human
flesh, Willem de Kooning's filleted women, art photographs of
men urinating in each others' mouths, brutal rap lyrics, or
truculent heavy metal. Sorry. So I believe in just some art: the
art of Pissarro, Caravaggio, Manet, Yeats, Shakespeare, Hardy,
Handel, Charlie Parker, Coleman Hawkins, Schubert, Mozart.
The one true art—and I've got the goods on it!

I believe in nature, believe that nature is good. As I have
said, years ago Suzanne and I replaced formal religion with
long Sunday-morning walks in parks or the countryside—a
form of prayer. Perhaps these strolls are as close as I will get to
a discernible God. When we walk far enough, nothing matters
but animals, birds, and trees, houses and outbuildings tucked
into windbreaks, the paths responding to each fold of the land,

our dog striking off into fields and woods. My joints grind and aging muscles become wayworn, but somehow I never seem to grow older on these walks. I believe firmly in them. I love striding through effusions of seeds, insects, rain, snowflakes, or stars at night. Even when we travel we seek places for our strolls.

On a damp Sunday morning in London fifteen years ago I stepped out of our small hotel to buy a *Times* and wished I had worn my raincoat. Suzanne was waiting for me in the breakfast room when I returned, and we ordered soft-boiled eggs. I told her that the walk we planned in Green Park was going to be a bit moist. I had just bitten off a piece of toast when I felt a sneeze coming on. Before I could swallow, I had to suddenly draw in air and the morsel was sucked in, lodging firmly in my esophagus. At once, I knew I was in trouble.

I made a noise like a trapped mouse and Suzanne looked up from the newspaper. I pointed to my Adam's apple as my eyes began bulging. I stood up and moved away from the table, still relatively calm, believing that the situation would momentarily correct itself.

Suzanne stood with me, announcing to people at surrounding tables, "I won't be good at this. Can any of you help?" She came up behind and tried unsuccessfully to give me a Heimlich maneuver as the other diners turned away in alarm. A waitress ran for a glass of water. No one else came to help. I was heaving violently for breath. Once again I was choking on bread, perhaps my last communion.

People began rising from their tables and backing away, several hastening out of the room. I did not wish to inflict this spectacle on them. It was happening very quickly. I had a strange, alien thought—almost a musing. So this is *it?* How silly and tawdry. It would be embarrassing to die in front of all these people, but I knew that if I could not breathe soon I would be finished. My vision was dimming. I turned to face the wall, fighting for air, seeking some kind of privacy for my death. I was seconds away from unconsciousness, the umbra deepening.

I want so very much to say that, at that point, I saw a beckoning nimbus, a vision of angels and sounds of supreme music. But I cannot. All I recall is descending gray light, going to darkness, a place I would turn away from if I had a choice.

Before I collapsed completely, a voice came from behind me, a small American voice of authority. She told Suzanne to go to the desk and order an ambulance, getting her out of the room. "I think I can help," the voice told me. "Sit down in that chair." I sat without hesitation and arms encircled me from behind, just below my rib cage. There was an abrupt exertion of pressure and the piece of bread popped out. I gulped air and almost wept with relief. "Relax and breathe evenly," she said.

She was a nurse from Tennessee on a tour with her sisters, a small woman in a pink jumpsuit. If she had not been in that breakfast room that morning I would not be writing this, but she gave me a sudden, expert compression and I was able to go on with my life. For years I sent her boxes of apples from our Wisconsin ridge top at Christmas and exchanged notes with her. I sent her a copy of my selected poems. I lost touch with her when she retired to Florida, but I will never stop being grateful. In our occasional exchange of notes, I discovered she was a devout person, happy that she had been able to save my life, believing that God had intended it.

I wish I could witness for her, and for myself, that I saw imminent glory as I neared the death she saved me from. Instead I saw a wall of dim coldness. But perhaps it was a door that was about to open. Beyond this door the light was radiant and divine. Maybe there was a long path through lambent autumn trees where I could walk forever.

Spring

ALTHOUGH I WAS NOT SUSTAINED by formal faith, the damage to my spirit caused by the abrupt conclusion to my publishing career began slowly to repair itself. By spring I began to realize more fully that the countryside had become our home. When the thaw started, the fields began to unlock and grow moist. Our road was glutinous. There were many tracks in the mud. Plants and trees were poised, hinting at green, but there was no lusty, verdant unraveling yet. It was a landscape full of hints. I loved the feeling of newness and potentiality. It was exactly what I needed.

At last we had time for horticulture. We strongly felt the urge to start our garden, wanted to put seeds into the ground, but already I had "buried" our cultivator and had to tug it out of mud with the truck. We were excited and overanxious. Richie Halverson stopped by to say he couldn't fertilize our fields yet because his tractor would get stuck in the "greasy" earth. I didn't tell him about our cultivator. I was embarrassed into patience.

There were still patches of old snow and little trickles and runoffs in the woods. The migrating birds hadn't arrived yet, just hawks and crows, and the chickadees, flickers, woodpeckers, cardinals, and blue jays that still came to our feeder. It was not so cold as to be uncomfortable, but too early and damp for real warmth. In the woods we smelled strong odor of skunk and hoped that Sheba was taking note. She had been sprayed three times by the same skunk the previous summer, and we didn't wish to start making runs to the store for tomato juice.

Early spring is a time for natural faith. The land looks scrappy with sodden residue of old vegetation and the grass is still brown. There are dingy drifts and gravelly piles of snow left along the road by the plough, but things are stirring and rooting underneath. I began to feel the urgency in the air. Bitterness is boring and debilitating. If I could not forgive, I could at least look ahead to the real concerns of spring. To become involved in this is elevating.

Buds on the trees begin to tentatively unclench, not committing themselves completely, but still signaling intentions. Garden bulbs unroll their stems and lift their exotic heads. There are multitudinous delicate blossoms in the woods and fields; they are like stars—the longer and closer you look, the more you see. Violets are elegant, purple, and some are albino with reverse coloring and shading. Buttercups, jack-in-the-pulpits, pyrola, blue-eyed grass, gentian, and aster. Then flowering trees—wild plum, apple, mulberry, dogwood, wild cherry, chokecherry, elderberry, crabapple—no longer able to control their exuberance, begin to display blossoms in full.

Dandelions become radiant in the yard and fields. They are such happy, buoyant plants. I cherish them and cannot understand why people dislike them. Decades ago, walking home from school, I was dazzled by a whole bank of newly sprung dandelions. They seemed to a first-grader like bright treasure, and I excitedly gathered a large bouquet. They had just bloomed that afternoon and their yellow dust warmed my knuckles as I picked them. I carried them home in my empty lunch pail as a love gift for my mother. We put them in water, but they turned brown almost immediately. Nevertheless, we kept them, bedraggled, for weeks on a shelf above the breakfast table for what they symbolized. Dandelions are such generous plants, free with their brightness, edible in salads when they are fresh, pleasantly fermentable when their blossoms are young, presenting a pleasant dry white wine. Years ago people even used the autumn roots as a laxative.

In late spring, birds are crazy with love, chasing each other and coupling in the grass, along the roads, sometimes even in the air. It is damned exciting, this aerial display of hormones, very warming even to a sixty-six-year-old man.

I become overactive and sometimes careless in the spring. The previous autumn I had dropped some dead elms to be sectioned and split for firewood, and we laboriously dragged the brush out of the woods into the field to be burned in the spring. Several rabbit families had assumed the brush pile for winter shelter, and they were nesting now. We came, heedless, with our matches and old newspapers at dusk to start the fire; we were tired, thinking about our waiting drink and dinner, unaware of the residents in the sticks. The adult rabbits sprang away in alarm when we approached. We did not realize they had abandoned their nests. Probably they had tried to move a few of their young when we first approached, but we had not observed them. Most died in the intense heat of the burning brush, but some crept out of the brush on their own, near naked and blind. When we saw them we realized what we had done. We comforted ourselves by believing they were at least safe from the fire, but then as dusk descended and the fire grew brighter they began to creep back toward the light and warmth. It was the only home they knew. They were entirely vulnerable now.

As I gazed numbly into the fire, I thought I heard a shrieking noise. I wear hearing aids and have had tinnitus since my army days, so my ears ring constantly. Suzanne said, "I think you've stepped on a baby rabbit." My heavy work boot had crushed out its intestines; its small head was thrown back and its throat open. I reeled, despairing, horrified, feeling shamed and brutal. Suzanne said, "Don't dwell on it. Put it into the fire. It can't be undone." For days I could not avoid the memory of the damage I had done, of how that small cry became the center of the coming night, piercing silence and darkness.

Summer

I AM NOT A FULL PARTICIPANT in the huge, vital activities of summer in the driftless hills, and I remain mostly an observer. There is endless work to be done on the farms, but if I tried to help I would be more trouble than I am worth. It is no season for rumination or indecision. The farmers hope always for perfect proportions of sun and rain. A few of them still watch the phases of the moon. But whatever is given, they must unhesitatingly make the most of it. Inexperienced help is a burden.

Summer is massive and inclusive. The heat is still and immense, but small breezes move across our ridge and give relief. We savor these puffs as if they were fine hors d'oeuvres. I loved hot weather when I was a boy, playing baseball, being a catcher endlessly under the sun, but old poets must be careful, and we spend most summer days under cover of trees or roofs.

At night the urgent tree frogs in low wet areas and cow ponds try to become the voices of the myriad stars. Legions of them spread in branches and grass in the warm darkness, calling to each other; some crawl up the door of my writing shack, perching on top in dimness where spiderwebs trap the gnats. When I open the door in the morning they fall down on my head and shoulders and I recoil from their chill, damp bodies.

I try to get to my shack in the early morning, working to the whir of an electric fan before the heat mounts. On our walks we amble slowly, dip down into the shade of the woods to feel the cooling spray of trees. Sheba pants and drinks water. Because we do not like the air-conditioning, we usually sleep out of the sheets, reading late until things have cooled down before turning off the lights.

We hear distant tractors sometimes at midnight in the summer, at four in the morning or ten in the evening, under starlight, even in rain. Far off, farm machines hum in the valleys and on the ridges, encroaching on the silence. Richie Halverson suddenly appears in one of our fields with his cutter bar at five in the afternoon to "take chop." He runs three stripes of hay, blowing the loose grass into a wagon, then he disappears for days. He appears again a week later and takes down a whole field of alfalfa and clover. The next day he comes with his rake and tractor and windrows the hay into perfect rows. A hired tractor pulling a squat baler appears late the next afternoon, straddling the rows and swallowing the lines of hay. Periodically it stops like a great, fat field bird to give a shake and shimmy, laying a large, blond, perfectly bound bale like an egg. At twilight, the bales begin to look like groups of standing stones on the Salisbury Plain.

Richie toils on his own farm constantly. He keeps all this work and movement in his head. He seems a driven animal in the heat. We wave to him as we pass him on his tractor. Wisconsin farmers have a special mode of greeting. They slowly raise two fingers from the wheel as they pass you. We call it Norwegian cool. The French farmers near our house in Puivert look incredulous if you wave to them, and they do not return your greeting. The hippest farmers in Wisconsin raise only one finger from the steering wheel when they pass. I cannot presume such a prerogative. Mine is a two-fingered greeting.

In a late afternoon I sometimes stroll out into a hot field, raise two fingers to Richie on his tractor, and hand him a can of cold beer. It seems the best thing I can do and makes me feel at least a bit like a participant. Richie always courteously switches off his motor to chat a bit, although he really wants to keep going. When he's finished with this chore, he has to get his cows in for milking, then after supper he will be in bed by nine.

"How's it going?" I ask.

He pops his beer and tilts back his Chicago Cubs hat. He is ruddy from the sun; his Norwegian skin does not tan. Despite the umbrella he has mounted on his tractor, his hands and face are like sides of beef. "Not too bad. Corn seems to be okay, but I wish we'd get some rain. It's going to start tucking in if we don't get a few showers. Them grasshoppers are in again. They like it dry. Squeeze the juice right out of clover blossoms. You seen any deer? My rake threw a couple prongs and I was down for half a day last week. I don't need that this time of year. You know that old tobacco shed on Will's place? I kept my backup cutter in there so I could get to Will's hay easily. Other day he calls and says it's collapsed. Just fell down in daylight! No wind at all. Dented the heck out of my bar. I had the dickens of a time explaining to the insurance people how this could happen on a nice day. You see that lightning the other night? Hit one of my bales up in the old double field. I saw the smoke in the morning and found it burning. Snapped one of my cows, too, one of my good ones. I hope she makes it. What the hell! Why can't it hit one of the old bossies, if it's going to do something like that? You see that All Star game on TV? Boy, they make them things last a long time. I had to go to bed by the fourth inning. How you folks doing? Grandkids coming in? We're real good, thanks." Richie's poetry.

I tell him I don't want to be holding him up from his work anymore and he reaches for his switch; the ignition pops and kicks on. He is a master mechanic, a brave, energetic, important man, master of many crafts. He gives me a grin and a slight lift of one finger, then reenters the vastness of summer. I go back to our library and sit down with my book again.

On July 4 we always carry a blanket or folding chairs and mosquito repellent out to the old water pump, which marks the highest place on our land. From that rise we can see the distant fireworks shows, spurting and crackling simultaneously above the treetops from four different towns—Gays Mills, Seneca, Eastman, and Readstown—an American spectacular and a symbol of independence that somehow puts our lives into context in summer on our ridge.

The Catcher

I just wanted to catch.
It was the only thing I wanted to do.

Del Crandall

SUMMERS IRRESISTIBLY TURN ME to baseball. It is my old habit, an intrinsic disease for which there is no cure. But mine is a curiously hybrid strain of this great American affliction. Catching is my passion.

At lunch with friends a few years ago when I was still living in Iowa City, we were recalling the irreplaceable delights and challenges of playing baseball. All of us were well over fifty, wearing our neckties and hard shoes. The talk grew ecstatic as we recalled the pleasure, and ultimately we challenged each other. Could we still play baseball? We decided we could at least play catch. I offered use of the large yard beside the stone house that was the press office. We agreed to meet the following Wednesday. I went home that night and thrashed around in our attic until I found an old catcher's glove. Suzanne grew silent and worried when I brought it downstairs. I tightened the laces and oiled it at the kitchen table. "Don't get hurt," was all she said. The next Wednesday I tingled all day in the office until we met late in the afternoon.

We started slow, just tossing at about twenty feet. But soon we were backing up, and the gloves began to pop a little. I even got down in my catcher's squat a couple of times for less than a minute. The memories were rolling for all of us. We groaned when we stretched, threw stiff armed, and only slapped at low throws with our gloves. Cars stopped on the street and drivers were incredulous.

No one got hurt, but we were tired after twenty minutes, ready to go home in half an hour, thirsty for beer, headed for our easy chairs and the evening paper. We were mightily pleased with ourselves and promised each other to do it again. We would work hard to get in better shape.

Suzanne had needed the car that morning, so I rode my bicycle to work. I slipped my catcher's mitt onto the handlebar and pedaled slowly home under the branches of the warm, tree-lined streets of Iowa City, my old Pittsburgh Pirates hat slightly askew—a sweaty, weary, sixty-year-old man, happy as a puppy with a biscuit.

In the early autumn of 1945, a great inquietude lifted from the world. The war had ended that summer, and adults seemed happier and more relaxed; even the life of an eleven-year-old boy was less restricted. My parents allowed me a rare day off from school to keep my father company on a drive from Canton to Cleveland. The representative from Krippendorf Foot Rest Shoes was in the territory to take advance orders for the spring line.

Jesse Drew was a skinny, mothlike man with a gray-yellow moustache. It was warm in his hotel room, so he flitted around opening windows when we came in. He'd already taken off his cuff links and loosened his tie. His big sample cases were open on the bed. Like most traveling salesmen, he was a man of good wit. Every year at Christmas, Jesse Drew sent our family a large box of fancy almonds with the same note: "Comes the time of year when I can say, Nuts to you!"

As my father and Jesse Drew worked on the order for our shoe store, I played a baseball game I'd made up with marbles and a pencil on the dusty hotel rug under a floor lamp. When my father finished his selection, he and Drew leaned back in their creaking rattan hotel chairs and talked about prosperity and baseball.

Drew noticed I had grown restless and asked me about school. He called room service, ordered two bottles of Pabst Blue Ribbon and a Dr Pepper. He brought out a bag of peanuts, and we all chatted for a while. He asked me if I liked baseball.

Oh, yes, I did, very much. I listened to the Cleveland Indians games with my father.

Did I want to be a pitcher?

No, no. I wanted to be a catcher.

A catcher!

Recently I had seen a picture of Birdie Tebbetts, the Detroit Tigers catcher, in pads and shin guards, his cap turned backwards, his glove at the ready, staring fiercely at the camera. I was smitten. I liked the idea of playing baseball and looking like a crusader.

Drew had noticed me playing my marble baseball game. "Jerry," he said to my father, "you ought to take this boy to see the Indians this afternoon. Bob Feller's just back from the navy, and I think he's scheduled to pitch." He picked up his copy of the *Plain Dealer* and smoothed out the sports section. "Yes, Joe Haynes for the White Sox. One o'clock. If you hustle, you can make it. Get a hot dog on the way in."

The nuns had taught me to pray for things I wanted. My father rarely made snap decisions. I was almost down on my knees when he smiled. As we left the room, Jesse Drew told me, "Watch how Frankie Hayes handles Feller's fastball. You'll learn more today at the ball yard than you would have in school."

The Indians abandoned League Park for capacious Municipal Stadium the next year, but in 1945 they still played weekday games in the venerable concrete and steel stadium. It was overwhelming to me, full of echoes and loud adults, vendors hawking pennants and peanuts under the crusty girders. The field was close to the stands, and you could see the players' faces, hear their shouts and curses. Feller was cheered loudly. He was fast and intense, but wild after four years in the service. The White Sox batters were jittery and walked away from the plate muttering.

But my eyes were mostly on Frankie Hayes, and on Mike Tresh, the White Sox catcher. I saw how they directed the game, gave signals, made decisions, how a catcher was the only one who faced everyone else on the field. I even studied how they lifted their masks to spit. They weren't stars, and they weren't spectacular, but they were the steadiest and most important players. They watched everything and caused things to happen. Lou Boudreau, the Indians' young manager, talked to Hayes as much as to Feller when he came to the mound to steady his pitcher. Hayes was a veteran workhorse. He had caught 155 games the previous year. He seemed central to every movement of the game. He even stepped out in front of the plate and directed Mackiewicz, Seerey, and Heath on where to position themselves in the distant outfield green.

The game went on a long time for an eleven-year-old, and in the late innings my attention drifted. I was thinking about being a catcher and what it might mean to my life. I never saw Jesse Drew again, but if I knew where he was in heaven, I'd send him a box of fancy almonds.

The summer after I watched Frankie Hayes at League Park, I began to learn firsthand what it meant to be a catcher. We went to visit my mother's family in Indiana. Uncle Joe, one of the enduring heroes of my childhood, was there. He had pitched professional baseball in the Three-I League as a young man, until he developed a sore arm and was sent back to the coal mines. But even in his middle age, Uncle Joe was still looking for a catcher—and suddenly, there was his nephew.

It was Joe who bought me a mitt, a wonderful purple-brown Rawlings Mickey Owen model. I loved to smell it and rub neat's-foot oil into its pores. At night I put a ball in the pocket, wrapped it with twine, and took it to bed. I wish I still had it.

I was twelve years old when Uncle Joe started tossing base-balls at me every evening after supper. First I dodged his pitches and then ran to retrieve the ball. He didn't scold me, and he didn't stop throwing. Eventually, I got tired of chasing the balls and started reaching out with the Mickey Owen to stop them. I took a few hard ones on the wrist, got a fat lip or two. Pain was my teacher. Soon I was really trying to catch the ball—almost in self-defense. Finally I did catch one. Then another. Uncle Joe beamed, and cranked up a little more. By the end of our visit he was heating up, putting some mustard on his pitches, and I was catching them.

That was when catching began to have its true meaning for me. From that day, I devoted myself to the practice. I com-pelled everyone I knew to throw baseballs at me. I thought of little else, took it indoors as well as outdoors. The catchers whose pictures I tacked to my bedroom wall looked so *significant* crouching in their armor like medieval knights. This image became an icon of my youth. I could not imagine any-thing more staunch and manly than a catcher down low, ready to do his important work—chivalrous, brave, and true in mask and armor. He was the guy who owned the game's his-tory and spirited everything on the field.

I badgered my poor father to buy the equipment until, piece by piece, I assembled almost a complete outfit. Lefty

Gomez once called the catcher's equipment "the tools of ignorance," implying that you had to be a little dim to play the
position. But I was brilliant in my persistence, acquiring everything but the mask. I begged and begged, but my father stood
his ground. We could not afford the mask—and that was *it!*

My parents had married and started our family in the
midst of the Depression. Like most people who went through
this trauma, they never quite recovered. My father particularly
remembered the bad times and felt his responsibility. Watching
pennies was a way of life. The mask would be an extravagance.

So I became a borrower. A knight with a mortgaged helmet.
In practice I had to cadge the alternate catcher's mask. In games
I had to make a deal with the opposing catcher so that I could
use his mask. My father came to games sometimes and
watched me scramble for a mask between innings, but he
never broke his resolve.

I stopped playing team baseball when I was nineteen, but I
have been a catcher all my life. Warehouse manager, technical
writer, soldier, bookstore buyer, editor, publisher, director,
husband, father, gardener, poet—I have borne the catcher's
attitude to all these tasks. I have given signals, received pitches,
watched the field, kept my eye on the ball, avoided most cheap
shots, backed up bases, chattered encouragement, made
decisions.

When I was young, life sometimes scared me, as death does
now. Catching was a way of dreaming a life I could live. Putting on that mask, I was as important in my play as an ancient
Greek actor was in his. I wasn't hiding behind the mask; I was
posing as something more real than real. Other players seemed
almost naked with only a glove on their hand. I wore armor
and gave directions. As Orestes said, I was "disguised as an
outlander, for which I have all gear." I spoke the veritable lines
that had been prepared by those ahead of me. I called for

illusions and tricks, planned retribution, witnessed triumphs and failure close at hand. I felt the pain of attack and schemed our defense. If I took off my mask, something serious was happening: we were either being assaulted and action was required, or our pitcher had been slain and new plans had to be formed.

When I could no longer actually be a catcher, almost directly I started trying to be a poet. The transition was natural: poetry was the only activity that felt sustaining and real enough to replace the physical act of catching. I was drafted into the army in January 1954, so the summer of 1953 was my last time on a baseball team. In the army I was alternately terrified or bored. I drank a lot of beer. Fortunately, I had an unlikely visitation from some benevolent god and discovered that I liked to read books. In a short time I discovered poetry, a preoccupation that has endured.

I began scribbling out my own words, laboring over lines and small poems. I could no longer be a catcher, but, I told my friends, I was going to be a poet. When I got home from the army, the photographs of Birdie Tebbetts, Sherman Lollar, and Jim Hegan came down and were replaced by pictures of Robert Frost, Dylan Thomas, and Walt Whitman. Catching had taught me how to approach poetry: patience, diligence, doggedness, alertness, and practice, practice, practice.

Through my childhood, an old-time catcher—a squat, hoary man named John Walters—lived in a large house around the corner from ours. He was well known as a fisherman, sports- man, and former athlete. Mr. Walters had two large cherry trees in his backyard, and every year I helped him pick his crop. When we were up on ladders in the branches amidst the ripe fruit, he would tell me stories about when he was a catcher in the early days of baseball, before the turn of the century. He caught barehanded. Recalling the sting of Uncle Joe's fastballs in the pocket of my padded Mickey Owen, I would peer through the branches at his large, liver-spotted, cherry-stained hands and marvel. He even claimed to have caught Cy Young when he was an amateur. Barehanded. Cy Young! But then my dad and I were reading a book about early amateur baseball and found that in those days catchers would stand well behind the batters and play the ball on a bounce, or even catch it off the backstop. Mr. Walters had left out this detail, but I still thought he was terrific.

Most of his talk was manly—strong talk about sports and work—but once he inadvertently showed me that even catchers are vulnerable behind their masks. He kept an old black-and-white pointer named Jack in a pen behind his house. Jack had grown old and stiff from Ohio winters, and his muzzle was pure white. One morning I hustled out to the back alley on my way to school and heard a strange, deep, rasping sound. I crept around Mr. Walters's garage and saw the old catcher—crusty, tough John Walters—sitting on the ground, cradling Jack in his arms and rocking him, his head high as he croaked to the old deaf dog, over and over:

Oh, Jackie boy,
Oh, Jackie boy,
My doggy joy,
Don't go away,
My baby boy.

Not much of a song, but pretty good for an old catcher.

In my meditations on catching, I fantasized that the position ran in my blood. My grandfather told me about a star catcher from his boyhood: Chief Zimmer was born in my home state, Ohio, and played nineteen years with a number of major league ball clubs late in the nineteenth century. He never made the Hall of Fame, but he hit .267 for his career and developed innovations in playing the position. He even patented an early baseball marble game. When he died in 1949, I clipped his obituary (with a picture) from *The Sporting News* and carried it in my wallet. He was an old-time guy with a melancholy face and a big, broken nose. I would show the clipping to friends and claim that Chief Zimmer was my great-grandfather. The obituary said that he used a piece of beefsteak in his small glove when he caught fastball pitchers. That made me glad to have the Mickey Owen.

But catching is a particular, personal passion and does not run in the blood. When my son was born in 1963, I made joyous phone calls to relatives, then went to a department store and bought two things: a stuffed purple cow that made a mooing noise when you pulled a string, and a Haywood Sullivan catcher's mitt. My son still has the purple cow. But like most healthy boys, he had his own dreams. Although he played third base very capably, he was never much interested in playing baseball. It no longer astonishes me to realize that he has turned out to be a wonderful human being who has achieved strength and character without donning the armor—shin guards, chest protector, and mask.

More recently, I have played catch with his son, my grandson, and have watched him grow stiff when the ball comes, turn his head and stick out his arm, then chase the ball down the road. Last year when they came to visit, he brought a battered catcher's mask that he had obtained in a trade with one of his buddies and wore it when we played catch. He knew I would be pleased. But it was an old mask, and it was too heavy for him. The other day my son informed me on the phone that Aaron has chosen not to play Little League baseball. He enjoys soccer more. He is also sensitive and humane, a bright, inventive student. Pain is not always a good or necessary teacher, and character can be built without crooked fingers.

But I spent my youth preparing for a catching life. At first my greatest difficulty was keeping my eye on the ball when a batter swung—I always turned my head when someone took a cut. Once during a pickup game, I found myself on all fours in the dust, as if lightning had struck me, a lump growing large on the back of my skull. Pain was my teacher again, and I learned there could be no illusions about this. From then on I willed myself to keep my head steady, my eye relentlessly on the ball. Thus catching compelled me to face things straight on.

When I was not practicing baseball as a kid, I was being a fan. My heroes were not the star catchers of those years—great ones like Roy Campanella or Yogi Berra—but obscure and less talented catchers on second-division teams: Bill Salkeld of the Braves, Jake Early of the Senators, Clyde McCullough of the Cubs, Al Lopez of the Pirates, Bob Swift of the Tigers, Buddy Rosar of the Athletics, Ray Mueller of the Reds, Les Moss of the Browns. I realized early that I was not of star quality, but I dreamed of becoming a steady performer, a solid, dependable catcher-worker like the good American folks in my neighborhood.

Canton was a mill town, a steel town, full of people who worked swing shifts. They were steady performers you could count on, like my father, who went to work six days a week in the shoe store, even when he was sick.

Needing practice, I recruited him into my scheme. I nagged him after supper until he put down his newspaper. Then we would take the gloves and ball out to the back alley. My father had curvature of his spine. I did not think much about this when I was growing up, but I think about it now. He had to have his suits and coats made specially, and he suffered back pains all of his life. Throwing a baseball was not easy for him. He worked hard to crank up fast throws so I could have a good practice, but he always wanted to quit before I did. When he started throwing underhand, I knew it was time to go in.

One morning after an evening game of catch, I heard groaning from the bathroom. When I opened the door, I found him on the bathroom tiles, his eyes rolled back in agony from the pain in his back. When he saw me he became embarrassed. He rolled over and pushed himself up off the floor, put on his pants, winked at me, and went off to work. I never asked him to play catch after this, but a few times a week he would come into my room after supper—smiling, carrying the gloves and ball—and say, "Hey, pal, let's have a catch." In a wonderful poem about his own father's devotion and suffering, "Those Winter Sundays," Robert Hayden asks himself: "What did I know, / what did I know of love's austere and lonely offices?"

One year I approached a local clothing store owner about sponsoring a baseball team in the Junior American League. He was willing, but only if I could persuade a presentable adult to manage the team. I approached our mailman, Cootie Lawson, who once told me he had played "semipro ball," tantamount in my mind to achieving the state of grace. Cootie agreed and soon had us practicing. I quickly discovered that he favored a stronger, older, more talented boy to be his catcher—but no matter: I would be second-string, the good journeyman waiting for his time to come.

Before long, however, I figured out that I was not even second in Cootie's eyes—there was still another ahead of me. Worse, we had only a dozen uniforms, and when the day came for the team to be measured for them, I was not on the list, despite the fact that I had arranged the whole thing. I looked again at the list to be certain. I even went back to check again after practice, to see if some mistake had been made. A few friends tried to console me, but Cootie never explained. I suppose there was nothing to explain. I took a long time walking home by myself through the park. I did not cry, but fifty years later this memory still pains me.

No matter still, I would stay and be the third-string catcher without uniform. I bought my own cap, approximately the same shade of red as the team's, although it did not have the team letters on it, and I stayed around to help. I "hung in there." I warmed up pitchers and chased foul balls. Game after game, I watched and waited. I kept my mouth shut and kept trying.

One day the regular catcher did not show up and in the third inning the second-string catcher hurt his leg sliding into third. Cootie turned around, and there I was. I strapped on my pads, borrowed the mask, went out on the field, and did the job. We lost the game, but Cootie bought me a Tastee-Freez along with the rest of the regulars. The next day I opened the local paper and found my name listed in the game box score:

	AB	H	R	E
Zimmer, C	3	0	0	2

I was verifiable. I was immortal. You could look me up.

In 1948 Miss Bicksell, a young speech and debate teacher, joined my high school's faculty. A recent graduate of Oberlin College, she was proud, poised, full of talk about art and culture. She had acted in plays and had theatrical mannerisms. When she was introduced to the student body, I was stunned— I had never seen anything like her before. She stood tall in her tailored suit and spoke with perfect diction. She was pretty and, as we used to say in those days, she was built. I immediately signed up for speech and for a short while forgot about catching.

There were plenty of good students in the class, and from the first day, she favored them. Two or three klunky boys became the foils, and I was the klunkiest. Much to the amusement of the good students, I became paralyzed with fear when I tried to give a speech. Miss Bicksell may actually have tried to be patient and understanding, but she must have found me a serious challenge. I wanted to impress her, so I selected as topics the only kind of art and culture I knew: Frankenstein movies, Mario Lanza, Norman Rockwell, Bishop Fulton J. Sheen. During one presentation I became so shaky that I actually collapsed to my knees. I looked up to see her bent over the desk, hand on her mouth, trying to hide her amusement as the students howled. I knew then for certain that I had wandered into the enemy camp. Art and culture be damned! It was time for catching.

And so, for my next and final speech, I talked about the Cleveland Indians catching staff. I propped myself up against the blackboard and crammed my hands into my pockets to hide their shaking. I spoke of how Jim Hegan had inherited the catching slot from the venerable Frankie Hayes in 1946, how he asserted himself and settled in, well-backed by the capable Joe Tipton and Hank Ruszkowski. I talked about how Hegan played the position and described the subtleties of his performance. No one knew what I was talking about, but everyone recognized my authority. Even Miss Bicksell. I made it all the way through and sat down.

The next day she took me out into the hall and told me that I hadn't talked about anything "particularly important," but she was pleased I had selected a topic I was familiar with. Earnest and stern, her helmet of brown hair fetchingly unruffled, she went on to say that, because of this speech, she was not going to fail me. When I saw my D+, I knew that catching had saved my bacon again.

I took deep pleasure even in the sensations of catching. When a batter took a cut and missed, it was good to feel the ball crack into the pocket of my glove. Like most young boys, I felt that I was being watched at all times—if not by other girls and boys, then by God and His angels. Behind the plate I imagined vast throngs of people applauding me, roaring like the wind in a sea conch. When girls were watching, I made a great show of squatting, shouting words of encouragement to my pitcher, snapping the ball back from my classy squat.

I was not particularly good at anything else. I was dreamy and mediocre in the classroom, too light and scrawny for football, too impatient to learn music. But I could catch. Never a star, but steady. I had moxie. I would be remembered—or at least I would remember myself—as a staunch journeyman, a dependable working guy. Catching was what I could do, and there was nothing more important. I constantly sought its essence.

The equipment remained fascinating to me. These days the catcher's mitt is big and floppy, like a first baseman's glove, and the pitch is snapped up in the web, away from the palm. Our mitts were like stuffed brown pillows shaped around a pocket consisting of several layers of leather that covered the palm. One of my enduring concerns was whether I could handle the stinging pain of catching a fastball pitcher. I wasn't going to use beefsteak. My father suggested a sponge rubber pad, but I took great pride in not doing this. Did Birdie use a sponge? Did Walker Cooper? Uncle Joe suggested that I dip my hand in brine before a game, but we didn't have any brine. My idea was that I could toughen my left hand for this punishment by pounding my right fist into my left palm. I did this constantly, to the point where people began thinking me odd. My mother asked me to desist at the dinner table; a teacher made me stop doing it in a study hall. But the pounding worked, and I rarely had trouble catching a fastball pitcher.

According to Bill Dickey's manual of catching, which I memorized more completely than my altar-boy Latin, a catcher should always catch with two hands. Until the ball gets past the batter, the right hand should be clenched into a fist to protect the fingers from foul tips; then it must be opened quickly in order to clap the ball firmly into the pocket as it hits the mitt on the left hand. Mickey Owen, the Dodgers catcher whose signature was on my mitt, became infamous for a pitch that he did not trap in his pocket, allowing a passed ball on a third strike, which led to the Yankees winning the World Series—a moment immortalized in a famous photograph of Tommy Henrich looking back and breaking for first as the frantic Owen charges after the ball.

The masks, formed of heavy-gauge wire or steel bars, were so weighty that my young swan neck ached after an hour of catching. Today's masks are made with light metal bars. Recently, some professional catchers have begun to use a new kind of brightly colored, over-the-head mask-helmet adapted from a hockey goalie's mask. It seems almost a desecration that something from a violent sport like hockey should be brought onto the genteel field of baseball.

In my playing days, the chest protectors that amateurs used had an extra flap attached to the bottom, fitting between the legs and over the crotch. I used to tuck this up under the chest pads so that I would look more professional. Once an infield umpire stopped a game and perfunctorily ordered me to untuck the flap. "Why?" I asked. "Because you're gonna take one in the nuts if you don't!" he rasped in exasperation. Now most chest protectors and shin guards are bright red. Catchers look like boiled lobsters behind the plate, more like Plastic Man than like Greek actors. The crotch flap has been replaced by the cup, which is worn out of sight inside the jock strap.

I constantly pondered and regularly practiced the art and duties of a catcher. I had a good arm, and my peg to second was "like a rope." I backed up the bases with gusto. I even

practiced chattering at the pitcher. Behind the mask, like
Ivanhoe encouraging his worthies, I imitated the strange,
almost sexual cant that older ballplayers used. "Come on,
Clete! Come on, you babe. Let's go, Clete. Come on, you guys.
A little chatter out there! We got this guy. Bring it in here,
Clete." I cherished the authority of giving signals to the pitcher,
making sure I hid my fingers from the opposition with my
mitt over the top of my crotch.

I worried and schemed about the "play at the plate," which
happens when the runner rounds third base and accelerates
toward home, where the catcher waits with a foot over the
plate, one eye on the ball coming in and one eye on the charging runner. A catcher is always vulnerable in this position, and
sometimes the action is violent. If the ball gets to him before
the base runner does, the runner's only option is to plunge in
and try to blast the ball loose from the catcher's grasp. Some of
the terrific collisions I witnessed gave me pause. I weighed less
than one hundred pounds until I was at least thirteen and was
never certain I could stand up to such appalling violence. Once
I saw Stan Lopata, the particularly rugged Philadelphia catcher,
make this play at the plate while he was a Terre Haute Phillie
in the Three-I League. A base runner rounded third at full clip
and streaked in, intending to crunch Lopata and jar the ball
loose. His triumph was not to be: instead of flattening Lopata,
the runner bounced off him as if he had slammed into a boul-
der. As he lay broken in the dust, Lopata—for good measure—
jumped on top of him, crushing him with his armor while
jamming the ball into his groin. I was certain that runners who
might collide with me would not be carried off the field like
Lopata's victim.

I decided I had to win these contests by craft instead of
brawn. My natural gifts were not physical. I might have been
wearing the tools of ignorance, but I was usually thinking. I
developed the technique of standing just in front of the plate

looking staunch, but leaving a clear path across. If the ball came to me in time I would leap upon the runner with tremendous show and tag him as he slid. But several times the runners came straight for me anyway in clashes that rang my bells.

A while ago my friend Franz Douskey mailed me a gift: an old Louisville Slugger #125, Genuine R17, Powerized, Jackie Robinson model bat. The knob is chipped in a few places, and the fat end is slightly frayed where someone left it propped up in wet grass for a few nights. There are nine circular marks in the wood where someone used it to pound in a pipe, but it is still solid and intact.

I took it out of the mailing tube and gripped the extra-thick handle in my hands, choking up ever so slightly. I stood up, made sure I was clear of Suzanne, our lamps, and the dog, and swung it—not hard, but snapping my wrists and arcing it. My stiff arms and shoulders pulled a little as I went around, but it felt wonderful. I swung it again and knew that, with this bat, I could still hit .234 in the Junior American League.

Catchers need to be catchers first. If they can also hit, that is a considerable plus. I had some raps but rarely bombed the fences. I worked at my hitting as much as I could but never improved it. All winter, every night after supper, I swung at a cork suspended on a string from the pipes in our basement. I put quarters beyond number into the batting cage at the local driving range. I was assiduous when I took batting practice, but though I would swing and swing, I could never master the true hitter's sweet rhythm, never see with his glittering eye, never stride with his marvelous, lethal step, never hear that swish, that resounding, satisfying crack.

But I had a few good whacks, and they were always with the Jackie Robinson model. The trouble was that I kept breaking them. I would glue and tape them back together, but then they would shatter. Then I would have to buy another, and it took me a long time to get the money together. I think altogether I had three. In between I labored with other players' lumber— Ted Williams, Ralph Kiner, Johnny Mize models—all too thin of handle, too heavy and ungracefully ponderous on the fat end for me. The Jackie Robinson was my stick. I am sure I could have raised my lifetime average twenty points if I had been able to keep myself supplied. Who knows what could have happened?

Now, thanks to my friend, I have this one. I keep it on a shelf in my writing shack. Whenever I look up and see it, I stand and pick it up. I don't always swing, but I grip it as though I am going to, trademark up, enjoying the balance and potential.

But I was a "fielding catcher," not a force with the bat. I let others put numbers on the scoreboard while I guarded the gate in my armor. After nine innings, even though you couldn't see it on the scorecard, I was as important as anyone.

Catching was twenty-four hours a day and twelve months a year for me. One winter the men's club from St. John's, our parish, sponsored a "hot stove league" appearance of some Cleveland Indian players. I was thrilled to learn that Joe Tipton, the reserve catcher who backed up Jim Hegan for many years, was to be among them. He came with several premier play-ers—Lou Boudreau, Larry Doby, and Bob Lemon—who got all the attention, but I watched only Tipton, noticed his large hands, his great sweating head, his protruding jaw, which he ground against his upper teeth.

He was not in a good mood that night, but I decided to approach him and ask for his autograph. I came up on his left side and he signed my program. I got another program, tucked my head down, and approached him from the right, hoping he would think I was a different boy. Then I put on my stocking cap and went straight up to him. I wanted to cheer him up

with my attention, make him feel his importance. Finally I
approached again from his left. At last he looked directly into
my shy, averted eyes, and drawled, "Why do you keep askin' me
for my autograph?" I was terrified, close to bolting, but held
my ground. I was standing before one of my heroes. "Because
I think you're great," I stammered.

"Kid," he said painfully, "go sit down. I stink."

I persevered and eventually managed to play respectably in the
local leagues. I had two moments of triumph, remembered I
am sure only by me: Once I threw out two consecutive runners
trying to steal a base, and once, amazingly, with my Jackie
Robinson bat I hit two home runs in a game. And once—yes,
I have thought of a third—once we were playing the league
leaders, and a fair crowd had gathered to watch the game.
Somewhere in the middle innings, a batter tipped a ball high
into the air behind the plate. I always had trouble fielding high
fouls, and this was the loftiest I had ever had a chance at. I
snatched the mask off and tossed it away, tilted my head back
while groping the uneven ground with my feet, and tried to
judge the ball's rise and descent as it hovered high over the
backstop. I would look like a fool or a hero, but there was no
going back. The ball dropped and I lunged toward it. It landed
in the pocket of my mitt as if destined to nest there like a
warm egg. I looked around in triumph and met the eyes of my
girlfriend, who was sitting in the first row of seats behind the
wire mesh. She looked at me with pure admiration and affec-
tion, and each time I think of this, she loves me even more.

I have crooked fingers on my right hand from taking foul balls.
I showed them to my children when they were little and told
them how I got them, so they would know that their father was
a catcher. I also have a scar in my right eyebrow from the time
a foul tip broke through a cheap borrowed mask. How proudly

I bore these wounds, imagining they gave me identity in a world that otherwise rarely noticed me. I was neither handsome nor smart, but I was a catcher. I caught the hurlings of the most powerful young men without flinching; I faced every player as no one else on the field did; I told the pitcher what to throw, and if he lost his composure, I trotted with jaunty importance out to the mound to counsel him. In no other part of my life—then, since, or now—have I had such authority and visibility.

I think now of a man like Ken Silvestri, a reserve catcher for the Yankees and the Phillies in the late forties and fifties. Silvestri had the misfortune of playing with those teams when more talented catchers like Bill Dickey, Aaron Robinson, Yogi Berra, and Andy Seminick were also on the rosters, and so he spent all his years as a bull-pen catcher. His nickname was Hawk, and his beak was prominent. He played in only one hundred games in his ten-year major league career as an active player and batted two hundred times. But he hit five home runs and had twenty-five runs batted in, and his lifetime average was .217. He had always been ready. He even managed the Braves for three games at the end of 1967 after they fired Billy Hitchcock, but the team was distracted and lost all three.

I remember watching Silvestri in the midforties at Cleveland Municipal Stadium as he warmed up Joe Page, the Yankees' jaunty relief pitcher. More than two decades later I saw him again in Pittsburgh. He must have been in his early fifties. He was bull-pen coach for the Braves, still warming up pitchers, still working on his pension, still lifting his mask to spit after every four pitches. As the game droned on at Forbes Field, I watched only Ken Silvestri as he caught the fancy slants of some young reliever in the bull pen.

Some people pull triggers, clear-cut ancient forests, write television ads, or spend every day on the take. Ken Silvestri had spent most of his adult life playing catch with a baseball. Perhaps he was not entirely content with his lot. But if I had not been a poet and a publisher, had I been 95 percent more talented as a catcher, I think I could have lived such a life happily.

Dairy Days

ALL THE WORK done in the driftless hills is celebrated in venerable seasonal festivals. The commercial orchards in Gays Mills host the Apple Blossom Festival in the spring, and in the autumn the town throws the Applefest at the fairgrounds, with a flea market, exhibitions, craft booths, and a parade through town. People sit together drinking Old Style Lite and cider, eating brats, barbecue, apple fritters, and fry bread. The flea and craft fair is fraught with endearing junk. We always buy at least an annual roll of duct tape at a tool stand, and some local jams and jellies. One year I bought a battered Bill Freehan model catcher's mitt for five bucks and, the same year, hesitatingly, jars of beer and onion jelly, which turned out to be savory and pleasant.

We never tire of watching the parades. Every high school band in the area comes through squeaking and banging, along with trucks decorated by 4-H clubs and local businesses, and smiling politicians in secondhand convertibles throwing candy to the kids. Some of the local dairies even toss little plastic bags of cheese curds. A livestock hauler and a fertilizer man show their cleaned-up vehicles, and the volunteer fire departments bring their vehicles through with sirens blowing; the "jaws of life" truck always brings quiet awe to the crowd.

Soldiers Grove doesn't try to compete with the other small town by throwing an annual harvest festival. Instead it hosts a celebration in midsummer called Dairy Days, including a parade, carnival rides, tractor pulls, a slow-pitch softball tournament, and a dance in the Elks Club outdoor shelter. I don't know why they always hire a band with the biggest amplifiers in the county for the dance. Older people sit around picnic tables in the shelter, unable to converse because of the astonishing din, numbly staring at the young dancers pivoting around each other to cacophonous country music.

I had a friend who moved to the driftless hills. He bought an old farm that had been in the Halverson family for decades; it was the original homestead where Richie's aged parents lived. They had grown old and wanted to move to a small, more manageable dwelling in Soldiers Grove. After the purchase Richie continued to rent the fields from my friend for pasturing his cows. My friend was twenty years younger than I, and he was in love with a Wisconsin woman twenty years younger than he. That presented quite a spread, but she was talented and beautiful and he believed he could make things permanent.

When she left him he was desolate and alarmingly depressed. We spent as much time as possible sitting with him and talking. It didn't surprise us when he announced that he was going to sell his farm. It was too full of memories and painful shadows.

The Halversons had given my friend a good price on the farm because we had introduced him and spoken for him. Their only clear stipulation was that they wanted to keep the place out of the hands of Jake Yant if it were ever sold again. The Halversons had even tried to include this restriction in the sales agreement, but it was not allowed.

My friend left the driftless hills, and the very next thing he did was to sell the farm to Jake Yant for a profit. We found out when we drove in one weekend and saw Yant's cattle in the Halverson fields. I called Richie, who was in abject pain. We felt entirely helpless. The only thing I could think to do was to apologize for the meanness and ill manners of my friend. It didn't help. Richie's wife was nonplussed and chilly, but maintained a civility that amazed me.

We called my ex-friend and in no uncertain terms terminated our relationship, but of course it was much too late. I saw Richie's father in the grocery store in Soldiers Grove and tried to talk to him, but he said his hearing aid battery had gone out and he couldn't understand me. Richie's mother had a mild heart attack, and no one doubted that it was the result of her anguish over the sale. The damage was permanent and we felt responsible, like vandals in the countryside—as if we would be evermore the outsiders who could never be completely trusted again.

The summer after our friend's betrayal of the Halversons and us, a summer of grievous difficulties and treachery in Iowa, we went to the Dairy Days dance in the evening. The band specialized in Elvis Presley songs at top decibels. I had stuffed cotton into my afflicted ears, but the amplified guitars and fiddles still bore through to the center of my head.

We were strangers at the dance but tried to participate. Suzanne and I had just finished a turn around the floor when I spotted Richie sitting with his wife and some neighbors. Richie has his own hearing problems, his right ear deaf from a childhood farm accident. He was smiling, looking alert with his friends, but I knew from my own experience that this was his practiced charade. He couldn't possibly be hearing any conversation. Before the band struck up its emphatic rumpus again, I asked Suzanne if she would mind if I tried to get Richie off for a conversation. She went to chat with some acquaintances and I tapped Richie on the shoulder.

He looked up and smiled. "Can I buy you a beer?" I asked. He looked at his half-finished can and came close to saying no, but he is a neighborly man. He excused himself to the others as they stared at me, and we went off to the bar, then took our cans of Old Style Lite away from the noise, down the hill to where the slow-pitch softball tournament was progressing under the lights.

A middle-aged Italian man was pitching for a pizza restaurant team. His forearms were muscled and powerful, and his belly was prominent under his T-shirt. He was bald down to his ears, wearing glasses, and playing without a hat. With astonishing accuracy he heaved the ball underhand higher in the air than any slow-pitch softball pitcher I have ever seen and made it come down spinning dead center on the plate. Batters were struggling and mumbling to themselves. Sitting in the bleachers, Richie and I watched those pitches rise high into the night, through the field lights up into darkness, then plunge down again, reilluminated, to where the hapless batters flailed.

"How's a man ever going to get any of that?" Richie asked. We watched some more. I wasn't sure why I had wanted to talk to Richie. I knew I would embarrass him if I tried to apologize again. I guess I hoped at least to assuage my feelings of guilt. But now I could think of nothing to say.

We watched another batter wave helplessly at the Italian man's high arched lobs. He went into his elaborate windup ritual again as soon as the ball came back from the catcher, not giving batters time to think or adjust.

Richie could tell I had things on my mind. Without looking at me, he asked, "How you doing?"

"I'm having a hell of a time," I said without hesitation, surprising myself.

"What's the trouble?"

"Work problems," I said. "The people who work for me have turned against me."

"That's bad," Richie said.

Someone managed to awkwardly foul off one of the Italian's pitches, and the batter's teammates cheered encouragement.

"You worked with those folks a long time, didn't you?"

"Now they don't even think I have enough steam to walk around the block. Hell, I worked more than forty years without any problems. It's all going to end in a mess." I realized I was whining and grew ashamed.

"You wonder sometimes how people can act so poorly," Richie said. "That's one thing about farm animals. They don't turn on you. Even when you get older."

His simple decency and accuracy almost took my breath away. It made me feel very clumsy. "Richie, I'm sorry about what happened to you and your family," I blurted out.

Slowly he held up one finger. Then he took a pull on his Old Style Lite. "That's already done," he said. "You didn't know. We don't think about it anymore. Look at the way that guy winds up, like he's getting ready to heave a bale of straw. I wonder who made up this game. This ain't softball. Fast pitch is softball. But you've got to be young to play that game. That old guy is doing all right, though, but mostly he's just got a trick. Who the hell wants to swing at a pitch like that? It's like looking at the moon. The old people used to say it would make you crazy."

"Maybe that's the idea. Did you play ball?"

"I had to quit about twenty years ago. Didn't have time and didn't have the reflexes anymore. But I sure liked to play. Fast pitch."

"It's too bad we can't play ball all our lives. It would help."

"That guy out on the mound is doing okay. He's worked it out so he can play till he dies. I think he owns that restaurant.

Pizza and softball. He's got it down. I bet he'll still be playing when he's seventy. Not a bad life. It must beat farming," Richie chuckled and set his can down on a plank. "You gonna quit your job?" he asked.

"I'm going to resign and take early retirement. We're going to move up here permanently."

"That'll make you feel better. What are you gonna do? Get some cows?" He knew better than this; he was grinning as he teased me.

"I'm going to do some writing and I think I'll take a lot of walks."

"That'll be good."

"How're *you* doing?" I asked him. "You ever think about retirement?" Richie had coped with serious physical problems the previous winter. He had diabetes. It had been a worrisome, dry summer. He developed a stomachache and thought he was nursing an ulcer. Maalox made him feel a little better, but he couldn't hold any food and he kept getting weaker. They finally figured out that he had an obstruction between his stomach and intestines, and they removed it with surgery. Through the ordeal he tried to keep up with his work. "Cows don't take vacation," he said, but finally he had to hire some help.

The crowd suddenly erupted in cheers. The Italian man had struck out the side and come up to bat. He had just driven the first pitch far back into the darkness over the snow fence in center field. He trotted unsmiling around the bases as his teammates hollered.

"That guy's a slow-pitch softball machine," Richie observed. "He ain't going to lose." We watched him round third base to accept the high fives of his teammates.

Richie had just finished putting all three of his kids through college, his youngest daughter graduating that spring from the University of Wisconsin at La Crosse. They were beautiful children, but he never boasted. It was a major achievement, and he had been such a good father he'd run his string out. They were all headed toward careers in teaching or technology—none of them was going to stay on the farm. He was in his early sixties, ailing, and was going to have to make some decisions before long.

"I'm thinking a year or two more, then I'll get out. I'll probably keep a few heifers, but I won't want to be milking anymore after that. My equipment's wearing out and prices are beating me down. Now they got these super cows; they're getting into hormones and cloning. Too much for an old guy like me. I go to the Grange and the young guys do all the talking. They're jabbering about computers and watching market prices. If I tried to say something they wouldn't hear me. There's new ways for the young bucks, and old ways are for old people. You just wonder sometimes if all the new stuff is really going to make things better. Anyway, maybe I'll just ride my horses and be a gent." He cackled at this, but he was talking about giving up a dairy-farming life his family had lived for over a century. He had two horses and loved to ride them. I guess he was musing about being a cowboy, although he always wore his farmer's baseball hat when he rode.

The Italian guy was out on the field again, flinging the ball high up through the field lights into the dark and down again. His team was ahead one to nothing. He wasn't going to lose.

Richie said, "Say, Paul. I really ought to get back to the dance. Thanks for the beer."

We carried our empty cans to a trash barrel, then strolled up the hill together. The band leads were singing through their noses, a deafening version of "Don't Be Cruel." When we reached the picnic shelter Richie turned to me for a moment before he went off to be with his wife. He didn't shake my hand, but he gave me a quick grin. We stood looking at each other, two guys just winding down their "fools' lives." I am not certain what Richie said, but it sounded like "We'll figure it out." Then he turned and shuffled with his wobbly, diabetic step through the picnic benches full of numbed elders toward where his wife was sitting with friends.

I found Suzanne and we walked down the hill from the picnic shelter to our car through the temporary whirligigs, concession stands, and merry-go-rounds. When we drove out of the lights of Soldiers Grove the summer night was glistering and wafting fresh air through the open car windows. We didn't talk.

As we moved along the dark road I thought of a night the previous winter when I had come up to the farm by myself for a few days to escape the dismal, faithless atmosphere in my office. I had gone into Soldiers Grove to meet a friend for dinner at the Old Oak Inn and subjected him to a recitation of my troubles. He is a good friend and did his patient best to comfort me. After dinner I drove home alone along Highway C past heaps of deep gray snow along the road and was ashamed of myself for putting him through the ordeal. The starless night was heavy and sepulchral and the drive up the ridge to our farm seemed more like a journey into relentless gloom. I missed Suzanne and Sheba. Unable to read, I went to bed and lay in the chill darkness, feeling guilty about the state I had allowed my life to come to. Self-pity drains your soul. I found no relief but, eventually, blessedly fell asleep.

Now Suzanne and I were driving on the same road under brilliant stars, enjoying the warm night air. We have lived in many places and had many homes that seemed permanent— where we had good work, love, authority, family, health, confidence. Eventually we moved on from all of them, usually to what we thought were advancements, but occasionally to misgivings and disillusionment. Always it seemed we were working toward some final home that would be our last, peaceful crowning place. We have come to this beautiful place that seems a dream come true, yet somehow we arrived damaged and our very presence has already caused injury.

When I was young I wondered what wisdom was and if I would ever attain it. I remember reading a passage from Aeschylus in a paperback copy of Edith Hamilton's *The Greek Way:* "God, whose law it is that we who learn must suffer. And even in our sleep pain that cannot forget, falls drop by drop upon the heart, and in our own despite, against our will, comes wisdom to us by the awful grace of God." This seemed very profound, mysterious, and dramatic to me when I was a lad, but now perhaps I really know what the old Greek meant. Although wisdom is imperfect and sometimes painful, it is the best we can hope for.

It is possible that this farm will not be our final home, but it is the ideal we have worked for. If we must give way to age and leave it sometime, I want to do so in gratitude and without bitterness, causing as little damage and strain as possible to it and the people I love. This is the best I can hope for. We are glad to be even strangers in this beautiful place. I have no wish to give a "first syllable of valuable or even earnest advice" to younger people. Thoreau was right at the age of thirty: I have nothing to tell "to the purpose." Indeed, in the end I lost authority and allowed myself to be easily hurt. But maybe—as Richie Halverson might have said to me in the Soldiers Grove picnic shelter as the country band resounded—I'll figure it out at last.

Autumn

BY THE TIME leaves start to tinge in early autumn we have been full time in the driftless hills for almost a year. The freedom has been exhilarating. Now every morning I walk with Sheba to my writing shack and work for two, three, or four hours. It is an extraordinary luxury, a lifelong dream come true. For forty years I had to scramble to find time to write. Now every day I visit my texts for as long as I desire. I am still a mass of pink scar tissue from my final experience with work, but I am standing on my two feet and breathing well, eager for my favorite time of year.

I received a call from the University of Montana, inviting me to sit in their Richard Hugo Chair for Poetry the following spring. I felt greatly honored by this. It brought some significance to what I had been striving for my whole adult life. I had met Dick Hugo a couple of times over the years. Once he poked me in the ribs with his knuckle and in his gruff way said, "Zimmer, you've got the ticket." So now I was going to check it in. It made the coming fall seem even more promising.

I read somewhere that autumn foliage is turned on by a signal from outer space that tells the leaves to shut down their factories for the cold weather. This releases the color elements that they have always held. The article didn't say who or what was sending this signal, but I am grateful for the sender. Perhaps this is one of the best representations we have of God. In any event, I choose to believe it is a benevolent force with a warm hand on the switch and an eye for great beauty. Perhaps it is a powerful and kind mover, similar to the one that tells the vulnerable birds when to migrate in autumn, when to rise into the nocturnal jets a thousand feet above the earth and race at fifty to eighty miles per hour through darkness until sunrise, when they can descend to earth to rest, feed, and fuel their fires, these small, brittle creatures: warblers, thrushes, vireos, orioles, sparrows, shorebirds. Later the same benevolent force tells them when to grace us with their return in spring.

The birds are massing now and preparing to move across the sky. When you can watch every day, you see that the movement of the season is subtle and the changes are constant. The foliage begins tingeing in early September. Only isolated leaves tumble down for a while, but things are poised, with hints of brown, russet, and yellow. The insects become lethargic and seem intent on last-minute business to conclude their year.

In late autumn I sit on our deck in a warm jacket and gaze down into the valley. There is gossamer shimmering through the air in the sunlight, strung through the yellow and gold trees and ferns down into the valley. The sun illuminates small hatches of insects in the treetops and birds feed on them, swooping and flitting in the dying maidenhair and bright cobwebs. Above, the sky is inviolate, flawless and deep as a blank page, waiting for flocks of birds to rise and scrawl over the horizon.

There is a farmer on his tractor in the distant valley chopping his corn stalks, going back and forth, line by line in his field, lulling me toward a poetic catnap as he empties his cart and comes back for more. The trees on the ridges across the valley are bright down to the valley floor where the farmer does his ordered, symmetrical work. A long hump runs

through the middle of one of his fields, but he rides right over
the top of it. I wonder what caused it—soil buildup around
an old fencerow, a line of long-dead elms, an Indian burial
ground? I've not yet given up speculating on the history of this
place.

On a dazzling, blowsy autumn day we walk up the field
road to the double pasture. Wind hustles up the ridge to where
we are ambling. Sheba is scouting ahead through grass and
underbrush. As we come over the rise we surprise a doe standing upwind just a few yards from us in the field. She hasn't
heard or smelled us coming and holds in place. We are all like
the staffage of painters in this landscape—this doe, born three
years ago at the edge of woods on the south ridge; this dog
who arrived in our lives from God knows where; and we, who
have come through many years from many places. We stand
together for a moment as if woven into a tapestry. Then suddenly the wind jumps up, the doe arches away over the grass
with Sheba ripping after it in hapless pursuit, and the two of
us, still astonished, rejoice in our marvelous good fortune.

Paul Zimmer is retired from a long and varied career in the book business. He lives on a farm near Soldiers Grove, Wisconsin, and spends part of each year in the south of France. Eight books and four chapbooks of his poetry have been published since 1967, and his essays have appeared in many publications, including the *Georgia Review,* the *Southern Review,* the *Gettysburg Review,* the *Ohio Review, Crazy Horse,* and the *Great River Review.* During the past few years he has served as a writer in residence at the University of Montana, Wichita State University, and Hollins University.